AF598719

The Eternal Conversation

Rabbi Jonathan Sacks

THE ETERNAL Conversation

OU Press
NCSY
The Rabbi Sacks Legacy
Maggid Books

The original publication of
Letters to the Next Generation was dedicated in memory of

Susi and Fred Bradfield *z"l*

who, in their lifetime, instilled in their children and grandchildren a deep love of Judaism and the importance of its values. Their commitment to Judaism, the Jewish people, and to Israel has remained an inspiration to their family and to all who knew them. Their lives were "letters to the next generation." May their memory always be for a blessing.

The Eternal Conversation

First Edition, 2024

Maggid Books
An imprint of Koren Publishers Jerusalem Ltd.

POB 8531, New Milford, CT 06776-8531, USA
& POB 4044, Jerusalem 9104001, Israel
www.korenpub.com

Cover photo by Natalie Friedemann-Weinberg

The publication of this book was made possible through the generous support of *The Jewish Book Trust.*

ISBN 978-1-59264-689-0, *hardcover*

Printed and bound in Turkey

The Rabbi Sacks Legacy perpetuates the timeless and universal wisdom of Rabbi Lord Jonathan Sacks as a teacher of Torah, a leader of leaders, and a moral voice.

Explore the digital archive, containing much of Rabbi Sacks' writings, broadcasts, and speeches, or support the Legacy's work, at www.rabbisacks.org, and follow The Rabbi Sacks Legacy on social media @RabbiSacks.

This book is dedicated in memory of

Barbara and Richard Rosenfield *z"l*
("Baba and Pops")

who spent their lives serving Hashem with joy
and embracing those around them with love.
Their unwavering commitment to Judaism, Torah study,
and the Land of Israel became a vibrant chapter
in the eternal conversation that binds us across generations.
May their memory always be for a blessing.

We, the grandchildren of Barbara and Richard Rosenfield, are proud to present this collection of works by Rabbi Jonathan Sacks. Our grandparents were admirers of Rabbi Sacks and his teachings on Judaism, ethics, and morality. This collection is a tribute to their memory, bringing together pieces that were originally published separately.

Many in our family were first introduced to Rabbi Sacks' work *Studies in Spirituality* as a gift from our grandfather after the passing of our grandmother. Barbara was a brilliant beacon of love and kindness, a best friend to everyone, and always ready with compliments. Despite growing up in a non-Jewish town, she remained faithful to her religion and would charmingly persuade her non–Jewish friends to walk on Shabbat rather than drive, asking, "Wouldn't it be such a nice day to walk instead?" She went on to study at Northwestern University, where she met Richard, who was raised in a more secular atmosphere of 1940s Chicago. He was a true renaissance man, with a talent for quoting Tolstoy and Thoreau, riding horses, and excelling in the film industry. They built a beautiful Jewish life together — raising three children, ten grandchildren, and supporting a myriad of Jewish and philanthropic causes.

In Rabbi Sacks' work, we get a glimpse of what brought them together and gave their relationship such strength. We see our grandparents in Rabbi Sacks' balancing of reason and spirituality, in his emphasis on the importance of Jewish law in building community and the power of prayer and gratitude to bring God's presence into the material world. The rabbi's references to philosophers and incorporation of politics mirrored Richard's academic background, while his commentary on the Tanakh echoed Barbara's kindness and ability to see the good in everyone.

As we reflect on our memories of Barbara and Richard, we hope this anthology serves as a reminder of the values they cherished. The words and works of Rabbi Sacks are their lasting gift to us, one that we believe will continue to impact the Jewish community and the world. May their memory be a blessing.

CONTENTS

PUBLISHER'S PREFACE

Rabbi Lord Jonathan Sacks *zt"l* possessed and shared profound learning, moral depth, and sheer eloquence, making him a leading religious figure not only within contemporary Judaism but among people of all faiths (or none). Each meeting and conversation became a *shiur*, a lesson in how to look at the world and how to experience our relationship with the Creator. It is a great privilege for us, paraphrasing the talmudic adage, "to return the crown to its former glory" by continuing to perpetuate Rabbi Sacks' literary legacy.

We are especially honoured to publish his writings that were not previously published in book form, in a beautiful new volume such as this. The works collected here, originally produced as booklets, have characteristically stood the test of time and are as relevant today as when they were first distributed during his time as chief rabbi. It is our hope that this new volume gives a new generation of young adults a chance to discover these works.

We wish to express our appreciation to the Rosenfield, Friedman, and Lefkovitz families, who have joined together to dedicate this volume in memory of their parents and grandparents, Barbara and Richard Rosenfield. We are also grateful to our friends and partners at NCSY who have joined with us to publish this volume, and in particular Rabbi Gideon Black for his efforts in bringing these works to light and for his insightful foreword. As always, we extend deep gratitude to our friends at The Rabbi Sacks Legacy for their continued partnership, in particular to Joanna Benarroch and Jonny Lipczer, together with Lady Elaine Sacks and the rest of the Sacks family, for their continued support for our work.

Finally, we wish to add our thanks to our colleagues at Koren who have contributed to this work: Tani Bayer, Dr. Yoel Finkelman, Aryeh Grossman, Taly Hahn, Ita Olesker, Rabbi Dr. Daniel Rose, Nechama Unterman, and Rabbi Reuven Ziegler.

May Rabbi Sacks' memory and Torah continue to be a blessing for future generations.

Matthew Miller
Koren Jerusalem

FOREWORD

The name of this book, *The Eternal Conversation*, may be the most apt description of Jewish learning and education possible. Our Torah is a dialogue that transcends time and space – between God and the Jewish people, between teachers and students, and between parents and children.

Yet not all conversations have everlasting impact. Many conversations are lost to the winds of time, with their ideas fading before taking root. To ensure that wisdom is transmitted in a way that will endure, the terms of transmission need to be set. One of the most fundamental of these is that the student must have a healthy measure of reverence for the teacher. This reverence gives the conversation the necessary vitality to survive the test of time.

In *Pirkei Avot* 1:4 Yose ben Yo'ezer of Tzereda teaches that when studying Torah one should "become dusted by the earth of the Sages' feet." This beautiful image is understood literally in the commentary of *Avot DeRabbi Natan*, which instructs a student in the presence of a Torah scholar to "not sit at an even level with him...but to sit *on the ground* in front of him...to receive his teachings with the same reverence and awe with which our ancestors accepted the Torah at Mount Sinai."

I had the sacred opportunity to learn from my teacher, Rabbi Lord Jonathan Sacks *zt"l*, on hundreds of occasions, but in only three instances do I recall doing so while literally sitting at his feet.

The first was in February 2001 on Bnei Akiva's National Weekend, which brought together two thousand teens from across the UK for a Shabbaton in Wales, headlined by Rabbi Sacks. While a typical dinner at a Bnei Akiva Shabbaton would be animated by lively singing, it was challenging for us to generate *ruaḥ* with such a large crowd that evening. That was, until I turned to see Rabbi Sacks standing on his chair next to me, singing *zemirot* with all his might. As we looked up at the sight of our revered chief rabbi, in his impeccably tailored suit, jumping up and down on his chair in song, we were left with no choice. Within moments we were all up on our chairs – no one remained seated. Once Rabbi Sacks had the crowd fully engaged, he scanned the room to find that the only people not on their chairs singing were the Welsh policemen serving on his security detail. He promptly insisted that they too find chairs to stand on and clap along with our singing.

Rabbi Sacks may have been best known as a teacher for his erudition and eloquence, but he recognised that for Torah to be transmitted to the next generation it needs to be shared with unbridled passion and vigour.

For a conversation to be eternal, it is not only the content of what is transmitted, but how it is transmitted that matters.

The second occasion was the following year in January 2002, the Shabbat of *Parashat Shemot*, in Jerusalem. British gap-year students spending the year in Israel convened at the Ramada Hotel for a Shabbaton with the chief rabbi. Rabbi Sacks used his talks during the Shabbat to encourage us to take on positions of communal leadership during our university years, upon returning to the UK following our studies in Israel. He made the case that we had a personal responsibility to use the Torah we were studying in Israel to enrich the broader Jewish community – the majority of whom may not have had the Jewish education we were blessed with. During his keynote talk, we sat in concentric circles on the floor of the hotel ballroom, hanging onto his every word. Rabbi Sacks described Moses stepping out of Pharaoh's palace, seeing the suffering of the Israelite people. Despite having grown up in royal luxury, Moses instinctively identified with his enslaved Jewish brothers and sisters. Rabbi Sacks quoted Exodus 2:11–12:

> It was in those days that Moses grew up, and he went out to his brothers and saw their suffering. He saw an Egyptian man striking a Hebrew man, of his brothers.
>
> And he turned this way and that, and he saw no one was there, so he struck the Egyptian and buried him in the sand.

"How could it possibly be that there was no one there?" Rabbi Sacks thundered at us. "Outside the royal palace in the midst of a bustling metropolis?! Of course there were people there! But there were no leaders. There was no one else who had the moral courage to stand up for the weak and oppressed, and so Moses recognised he needed to heed his calling and take responsibility for his people, no matter the consequences."

Rabbi Sacks quoted Hillel's charge in *Pirkei Avot* 2:5 that "in a place where there is no leader, strive to be that leader." Whether we would run a children's service in synagogue, teach in a Hebrew school, coordinate regular visits to a senior care home for Jewish elders, or share Judaism in any other way with our home communities – we were filling the vacuum of leadership that *Pirkei Avot* demanded of us. He insisted we reject a culture that views undergraduate years simply as a time for self-exploration, and instead asked that we use the time to share our Judaism with others. The sheer intensity with which he charged us to take responsibility for the broader Jewish community left an indelible imprint on me and many of my peers that Shabbat.

For a conversation to be eternal, it must endow the student with the responsibility to continue the conversation with others.

The final time I sat at Rabbi Sacks' feet was in New York in November 2011 at the International Conference of Chabad *Shluchim*, which brought together nearly five thousand Lubavitch emissaries from around the world. Rather than watching Rabbi Sacks on one of the many screens positioned throughout the hall, I joined a few *shluchim* who were huddled on the floor in front of the main podium. Rabbi Sacks was mesmerising that evening. His magisterial address lit a fire in the hearts of the selfless *shluchim* to expand their work with increased devotion to the Jewish people. Rabbi Sacks shared with those gathered how the Lubavitcher Rebbe directly influenced his personal journey as a rabbi and leader at critical junctures in his life. Through one-on-one meetings at 770 Eastern Parkway and later through their written correspondence, Rabbi Sacks' life decisions were intimately guided by the Rebbe, just like the Lubavitch emissaries in the room that evening were guided by the Rebbe's legacy. The speech allowed the emissaries to see Rabbi Sacks as one of them, and as a result his words penetrated so deeply.

For a conversation to be eternal, the student needs to know that the teacher understands them and has sat in their place too.

Rabbi Sacks exemplifies for us these three ideas of how to ensure that our Torah conversations are eternal in their nature, that they indeed transcend time and space, and continue to bring meaning and inspiration. With this in mind, it is a profound honour to present *The Eternal Conversation*, which was originally published during Rabbi Sacks' lifetime as *Letters to the Next Generation*; *Little Books of Big Questions*; *Ten Days, Ten Ways*; and *A Judaism Engaged with the World*. These concise writings offered Rabbi Sacks' wisdom in a digestible format that could be enjoyed as a companion to synagogue services, or as an entrée for teens and young adults seeking to access the enchanting world of Rabbi Sacks' thought. Collecting them in this new volume, under this title, reflects our aspiration to perpetuate Rabbi Sacks' teachings and example for future generations.

In recognising the opportunity to bring together these publications into an organic whole as a tribute to the memory of Barbara and Richard Rosenfield, of blessed memory, the Rosenfield, Friedman, and Lefkovitz families are doing a great service to the Jewish people. They are ensuring that Rabbi Sacks' written legacy continues to be codified in a way that will be transmitted for generations to come. Much like students learn at the feet of sages, grandchildren find love and wisdom at the feet of their grandparents. Three of Richard and Barbara's grandsons – Michael Lefkovitz, Jacob Friedman, and Scott Rosenfield – have spearheaded this publication with grace and humility, and in doing so have brought great merit to their grandparents' memory and offered a treasure for the entire Jewish community.

This book is being published while the dark cloud of October 7th, 2023, continues to hang over the Jewish people around the world. Rabbi Sacks' voice is sorely missed at this challenging time. With Israel facing continuous physical threats from its neighbours, and antisemitism raging around the world, we may be tempted to perceive only our vulnerabilities. However, since the outbreak of the war, it is abundantly clear that the Jewish people worldwide stand strong and resolute and are connecting more to Jewish identity and Israel than ever before. Fundamentally, our strength has always been sustained by our commitment to our Torah and tradition, and there is therefore no better time to be bringing to light works of Jewish learning and wisdom.

Since its founding in 1954, NCSY has carried the mission of inspiring the Jewish future. Given this surge of Jewish identity since October 7th, it may well be that at no time in the seventy years since NCSY's founding has its work been more important. Books like this are critical assets in engaging teens and young adults in their Jewish journey. We are therefore particularly grateful to the Rosenfield, Lefkovitz, and Friedman families for bringing to a broad audience these writings of Rabbi Sacks. We are confident this new volume will further inspire the Jewish future, while adding a precious contribution to our people's eternal conversation.

Rabbi Gideon Black
CEO, Tri-State NCSY
June 2024 / Sivan 5784

LETTERS

This section comprises two booklets published by Rabbi Sacks to provide inspirational readings during the climax of the Days of Awe, the Day of Atonement itself – Yom Kippur.

The first, *Letters to the Next Generation: Reflections for Yom Kippur*, was published in September 2009 to coincide with Yom Kippur 5770, and offers reflections on key themes of Jewish identity, culture, and values. These reflections take the form of letters written by a father to his children who have just become parents. The characters are fictional, but the issues they raise are real.

The second booklet, *Letters to the Next Generation 2: Reflections on Jewish Life*, was published two years later in September 2011, coinciding with Yom Kippur 5772. These further reflections are also written in the form of letters, this time to two fictional Jewish university students. They explore themes of Jewish faith, values, and identity.

INTRODUCTION TO LETTERS TO THE NEXT GENERATION

Yom Kippur is the day of days, when we give an account of our lives. We reflect on what has happened to us and what we plan to do in the coming year. To help this process I've written some thoughts that may evoke reflections of your own, for each of us must make his or her own decisions and no one can make them for us.

I've cast them in the form of letters written by a father to his children who've just become parents in their own right. I've done so because it's a way of discussing the big decisions that shape the rest of our life for us and those close to us. They are fictional letters, but the issues they raise are real.

Not all of us are married; not all are blessed with children; yet we can each make a unique contribution to the Jewish people by the life we lead and the kindness we show to others. Rashi wrote: "The main descendants of the righteous are their good deeds." Every good deed is like a child.

The single most important lesson of Yom Kippur is that it's never too late to change, start again, and live differently from the way we've done in the past. God forgives every mistake we've made so long as we are honest in regretting it and doing our best to put it right. Even if there's nothing we regret, Yom Kippur makes us think about how to use the coming year in such a way as to bring blessings into the lives of others by way of thanking God for all He has given us.

May God bless all of us for the coming year. May He hear and heed our prayers. May He forgive us and help us forgive others. May He grant you, your family, and the Jewish people throughout the world a year of health and peace and life.

Jonathan Sacks
Tishrei 5770

LETTER 1:
The Most Important Legacy

DEAR SARA, DEAR DAVID, I am writing these letters to you as Yom Kippur approaches, because it's the day when we ask the deepest questions about our lives. Who are we? How shall we live? What chapter will we write in the Book of Life?

It's also a time to say the things we've left unsaid. The most important thing your mother and I want to say is that you are our beloved children. You have given us more joy than you can ever know. In all of life, you were God's most precious gift to us.

What inspired me to write these letters is the old Jewish custom that parents write their children *tzavaot*, "ethical wills." It's based on the idea that the most important legacy we can give our children is not money or possessions, but spiritual ideals.

I truly believe that. Give your children too much money or material gifts and you will spoil them. They will grow up unhappy and unfulfilled, and in the long run they won't thank you. It will damage them and your relationship with them. Tradition was right. The best things any of us can give our children are values to live by, ideals to aspire to, an identity so that they know who they are, and a religious and moral heritage to guide them through the wilderness of time.

Children grow to fill the space we create for them, and if it's big, they will walk tall. Ideals are big; material possessions are small. Ideals are what make life meaningful. People may *envy* others for what they earn or own, but they *admire* others for what they are and what principles they live by – and it's better to be admired than to be envied.

That is what Yom Kippur is about. Judaism sets the bar high. It's a demanding, challenging religion, but that is its greatness. If I were to define what it is to be a Jew, I would say it is to be an ambassador for God.

We were never asked to convert the world, but we were asked to be living role models of justice, compassion, *ḥesed*, and *tzedaka*. We are the people of the book, who put learning and study at the pinnacle of our values, to show that faith is neither ignorant nor blind. We were asked to live our faith, day by day, act by act, through the complex choreography we call halakha, the intricate beauty of Jewish law. Judaism is a religion of high ideals translated into simple daily deeds.

That's what we received from our parents. It's what we have tried to give you. It's what we hope you will give your children. Not expensive clothes or holidays or the latest mobile phone. These are distractions from life, not life itself. Life is made by what you live for.

I say this to you at this holy time because I've seen too many people make the same mistake. Their marriages fail or they have a breakdown in relationship with their children and they ask, "What did I do wrong? I gave them everything." True, but not true. They gave them everything *except* what mattered: time, attention, selfless respect, and genuine, ethically demanding, spiritually challenging values.

Ideals will bring happiness to you and your children.

LETTER 2:
The Price of Things and the Value of Things

SARA, DAVID, these have been tough times. Financial collapse, economic recession, and uncertainty ahead. People have lost their savings, their jobs, even their homes. What do you do in times like these? The best answer was given by an American politician: *Never waste a crisis*. You learn more in bad times than in good.

The Chinese ideogram for "crisis" also means "opportunity." Perhaps that's why the Chinese have been around so long. Only one language I know goes one further, and that is Hebrew. The Hebrew word for "crisis" is *mashber,* which also means a birthing stool. In Hebrew, crises are not just opportunities; they are birth pangs. Something new is being born. That's why Jews have survived every crisis in four thousand years and emerged even stronger than they were before.

What the financial collapse should teach us is that we were becoming obsessed with money: salaries, bonuses, the cost of houses, and expensive luxuries we could live without. *When money rules, we remember the price of things and forget the value of things.* That is a bad mistake. The financial collapse happened because people borrowed money they didn't have, to buy things they didn't need, to achieve a happiness that wouldn't last.

The whole of consumer society is based on stimulating demand to generate expenditure to produce economic growth. This involves turning genuine values upside down. Advertising creates a thousand blandishments that focus our minds on what we *don't* have, while real happiness (as *Pirkei Avot* tells us) lies in rejoicing in what we *do* have.

So in a curious way a consumer society is a mechanism for creating and distributing unhappiness. That is why an age of unprecedented affluence also became an age of unprecedented stress-related syndromes and depressive illnesses. The most important thing any of us can learn from the present economic crisis is: think less about the price of things and more about the value of things.

There was one moment in the Torah when the people started worshipping gold. They made a Golden Calf. The interesting thing is that if you read the Torah carefully you'll see that immediately before and after the Golden Calf, Moses gave the people a command, the command of Shabbat. Why that command, then?

Shabbat is the antidote to the Golden Calf because it's the day when we stop thinking about the price of things and focus instead on the value of things. On Shabbat we can't sell or buy. We can't work or pay others to work for us. Instead we spend the day with family and friends around the Shabbat table. In shul, we renew our contacts with the community. We listen to Torah, reminding ourselves of our people's story. We pray, giving thanks for all the blessings God has given us.

Family, friends, community, the sense of being part of a people and its history, and above all giving thanks to God – these are things that have a value but not a price. Or, to put it another way: A basic principle of time management is to learn to distinguish between things that are *important* and things that are *urgent*. During the week, we tend to respond to immediate pressures. The result is that we focus on what's urgent but not necessarily important.

The best antidote ever invented is Shabbat. On Shabbat we celebrate the things that are important but not urgent: the love between husband and wife, and between parents and children. The bonds of belonging. The story of which we are a part. The community that we support and that supports us in times of joy or grief. These are the ingredients of happiness. No one's last thought was ever, "I wish I'd spent more time in the office."

Hard times remind us of what good times tend to make us forget: where we came from, who we are, and why we are here. That's why hard times are the best times to plant the seeds of future happiness.

LETTER 3:
Being a Jewish Parent

SARA, DAVID, I want to talk about children. God has blessed you both with children. They are the joy of our life, as of yours. Enjoy them. Spend time with them. Play, learn, sing, *daven,* and do mitzvot with them. On nothing else will your time be better spent. The love you give them when they are young will stay with them throughout their lives. Like sunshine it will make them flower and grow.

Having children is more than a gift. It's a responsibility. For us as Jews it's the most sacred responsibility there is. On it depends the future of the Jewish people. For four thousand years our people survived because in every generation, Jews made it their highest priority to hand their faith on to their children. They sanctified marriage. They consecrated the Jewish home. They built schools and houses of study. They saw education as the conversation between the generations: "You shall teach these things repeatedly to your children, speaking of them when you sit at home or travel on the way, when you lie down and when you rise up."

They saw Judaism the way an English aristocrat sees a stately home. You live in it but you don't really own it. It's handed on to you by your ancestors and it's your task to hand it on to future generations, intact, preserved, if possible beautified and enhanced, and you do so willingly because you know that this is your legacy. It's what makes your family different, special. To lose it, sell it, or let it fall into ruins would be a kind of betrayal.

And that is the point. Today, on average throughout the Diaspora, one young Jew in two is deciding not to marry another Jew, build a Jewish home, have Jewish children, and continue the Jewish story. That is tragic.

Your mother and I didn't spend too much time talking to you about our own family histories. But the truth is that virtually every Jew alive today has a history more remarkable than the greatest novel or family saga. It tells of how they were expelled from one country after another, how they lost everything and had to begin again. They were offered every blandishment to convert, but they said no. They sacrificed everything to have Jewish grandchildren. And today when being a Jew demands almost no sacrifice, when we are freer to practise our faith than ever before, Jews are forgetting what it takes to have Jewish grandchildren.

So how do you hand your values on? By showing your children what you love. Rabbi Moshe Alshich, the sixteenth-century scholar, asked in his commentary to the *Shema*, "How do we 'teach these things' to our children?

How can we be sure that they will learn?" His reply? The answer lies in the verse two lines earlier: "You shall love the Lord your God with all your heart, all your soul, and all your might." What we love, they will love.

There are many reasons for the high rates of assimilation in Jewish life, but one is fundamental. We are heirs to several generations of Jews who were ambivalent about being Jewish. I don't pass judgment on them; neither should you. Between the 1880s and the 1930s they lived through an age of antisemitism. Then came the Holocaust. Who would blame anyone in those days for saying, as did Heinrich Heine, "Judaism isn't a religion, it's a misfortune"?

But we are long past those days. One of the greatest gifts you can give your children is to let them see you carry your identity with pride. Your mother and I tried to show you as best we could that for us Judaism is our legacy, our stately home, our gift from those who came before us, the greatest attempt in all of history to create a life of justice, compassion, and love as a way of bringing the Divine Presence down from heaven to earth so that it etches our lives with the soft radiance of eternity.

We can't live our children's lives for them. They are free. They will make their own choices. But we can show them what we love. If you want Jewish grandchildren, love Judaism and live in it with a sense of privilege and joy.

LETTER 4:
Jewish Education

SARA, DAVID, send your children to Jewish schools. They are the pride of our community. They are our best investment in the Jewish future. A generation ago, Jewish schools were often seen as second best. They were where you sent your children if they couldn't get in elsewhere. Today, rightly, they are a first choice for many. That is a tribute to their excellence.

But they are more than that. For Jews, education is not just what we know. It's *who we are*. No people ever cared for education more. Our ancestors were the first to make education a religious command, and the first to create a compulsory universal system of schooling – eighteen centuries before Britain. The Rabbis valued study as higher even than prayer. Almost two thousand years ago, Josephus wrote: "Should anyone of our nation be asked about our laws, he will repeat them as readily as his own name. The result of our thorough education in our laws from the very dawn of intelligence is that they are, as it were, engraved on our souls."

The Egyptians built pyramids, the Greeks built temples, the Romans built amphitheatres. Jews built schools. They knew that to defend a country you need an army, but to defend a civilisation you need education. So Jews became the people whose heroes were teachers, whose citadels were schools, and whose passion was study and the life of the mind. How can we deprive our children of that heritage?

Can you really be educated without knowing Shakespeare or Mozart or Michelangelo or the basic principles of physics, economics, or politics? Can you be an educated Jew without at least a basic familiarity with Tanakh and Talmud, the classic Torah commentaries, the poetry of Judah HaLevi, the philosophy of Maimonides, and the history of the Jewish people? Jews in Eastern Europe used to say, "To be an *apikores* (heretic) is understandable, but to be an *am haaretz* (ignoramus) is unforgivable."

My children, I hope we taught you enough to know that the first duty of a Jewish parent is to ensure that their children have a Jewish education. For almost a century, that whole value system was in disarray because Jewish life was in disarray. Jews were in flight from persecution, first from Eastern Europe, then from Western Europe, then from Arab lands. They were preoccupied by rebuilding their lives and ensuring that their children were integrated into the wider society. Jewish education was a casualty of those times. But not now. Today we've begun to recover something of the tradition. Yet our standards are still far too low.

The world is changing ever faster. In a single generation, nowadays, there is more scientific and technological advance than in all previous centuries since human beings first set foot on earth. In uncharted territory, you need a compass. That's what Judaism is. It guided our ancestors through good times and bad. It gave them identity, security, and a sense of direction. It enabled them to cope with circumstances more varied than any other people have ever known. It lifted them, often, to heights of greatness. Why? Because Judaism is about learning. Education counts for more in the long run than wealth or power or privilege. Those who know, grow.

"All you children shall be taught of the Lord," said Isaiah, "and great shall be the peace of your children." Give your children a deep and wide Jewish education and you will be giving them the peace of knowing who they are and why.

There are only two other things more powerful still. First, practise at home what your children learn at school. Children need to see consistency. Otherwise they become confused, and eventually rebel.

Second, *let your children be your teachers*. Over the Shabbat table, let them share with you what they have learned at school during the week. You will be amazed at the pride you give them because you have allowed them to give something to you.

LETTER 5:
On Being Jewish

SARA, DAVID, you may wonder from time to time why your mother and I care so much about being Jewish. It's a fair question, and this is my honest answer: somehow, long ago, Jews were touched and transformed by a truth greater than themselves.

They were the first to encounter God as a presence within yet beyond the universe. This changed everything, for if there is only one God and every human being is in His image, it means that every human being has non-negotiable dignity. It means that human life is sacred. It means that in some ultimate sense we are all equal. And if the universe is the free creation of the free God, then we, in His image, are also free. From this flowed the system we call morality and all it implies by way of personal and collective responsibility.

Jews were the first people to understand the significance of human responsibility and freedom, the first to conceive of a society of equal dignity, the first to understand that right matters more than might, and a whole list of other insights that eventually revolutionised Western civilisation. Judaism inspired two other religions, Christianity and Islam, that between them today count more than half of the six billion people on earth as their adherents. And even when Jews rebelled against Judaism, they did so in world-changing ways: Spinoza, the founder of political liberalism; Karl Marx, the revolutionary; and Sigmund Freud, the doctor of the soul. I think all three were profoundly wrong, but they were all profound.

And Judaism is as relevant today as it ever was. Non-Jews admire Judaism for our strong families and communities, our commitment to education and the excellence of our schools, the emphasis we place on *ḥesed* and *tzedaka,* on practical acts of kindness and generosity. The Jewish voice is sought on questions of medical, social, and business ethics. People respect Judaism for its wisdom and insight. It has integrity without fanaticism. It has strong principles without seeking to impose them on others. It has humour and humanity.

Of course, Judaism is demanding. There are so many laws, so many details, that you can sometimes lose sight of the big picture. It's like the first French impressionists. At first people could see only brushstrokes and confusion. It took time before they realised that Monet, Renoir, Pissarro, and the rest were capturing the play of light on surfaces and producing a whole new way of seeing. Judaism can look like a blur of laws and customs, until you realise that it's a whole new way of living. Halakha, Jewish law, is about translating the highest of ideals into the simplest of acts.

Here's the paradox: Most people think that more people would keep Judaism if only it were easier, less demanding. Why all the commandments, 613 of them? Wouldn't it be better if we made being Jewish simpler?

Let's see. Think of Pesaḥ, Shavuot, and Sukkot. Which of the three is kept, on average, by the greatest number of Jews? More people keep Pesaḥ than Sukkot. More people keep Sukkot than Shavuot. That's true wherever you go in the Jewish world.

Now ask, which is the most demanding? Pesaḥ is by far the most difficult. It involves cleaning the house, *kashering* the kitchen, using special utensils, and much else besides. Next comes Sukkot. You have to buy a lulav and etrog. You have to make a sukka. Easiest by far is Shavuot, which has no special mitzva, unless you count staying up late on the first night for a *tikkun*. So, *the harder a festival is to keep, the more people keep it.*

Now think of the hardest day of all, one in which there is no eating or drinking, no joy or celebration, on which you spend the entire day in shul, thinking of all the things you did wrong. A perfect formula, you would have thought, for making sure that no one keeps it at all.

But of course the opposite is true. Yom Kippur, when all these things happen, is the day on which more Jews come to shul than any other in the entire year.

It's counterintuitive but true: *The things we value most are the things that are the most demanding.* That's true of study, it's true at work, it's true in sport, and it's true in matters of the spirit. Things that cost us little, we cherish little. What matter most to us are the things we make sacrifices for. If Judaism had been easier, it would have died out long ago.

Never doubt that it's a privilege to be a Jew. Head for head our people have done more to transform the world than any other. There are easier ways to live, but none more challenging. God asks great things of our people. That's what made our people great.

LETTER 6: Jewish Wisdom

DEAR SARA AND DAVID, wisdom is free, yet it is also the most expensive thing there is, for we tend to acquire it through failure or disappointment or grief. That is why we try to share our wisdom, so that others will not have to pay the price for it that we paid. These are some of the things Judaism has taught me about life, and I share them with you:

- Never try to be clever. Always try to be wise.
- Respect others even if they disrespect you.
- Never seek publicity for what you do. If you deserve it, you will receive it. If you don't, you will be attacked. In any case, goodness never needs to draw attention to itself.
- When you do good to others, it is yourself, your conscience, and your self-respect that will be the beneficiary. The greatest gift of giving is the opportunity to give.

- In life, never take shortcuts. There is no success without effort, no achievement without hard work.
- Keep your distance from those who seek honour. Be respectful, but none of us is called on to be a looking glass for those in love with themselves.
- In everything you do, be mindful that God sees all we do. There is no cheating God. When we try to deceive others, usually the only person we succeed in deceiving is ourself.
- Be very slow indeed to judge others. If they are wrong, God will judge them. If we are wrong, God will judge us.
- Greater by far than the love we receive is the love we give.
- It was once said of a great religious leader that he was a man who took God so seriously that he never felt the need to take himself seriously at all. That is worth aspiring to.
- Use your time well. Life is short, too short to waste on television, computer games, and unnecessary emails; too short to waste on idle gossip, or envying others for what they have; too short for anger and indignation; too short to waste on criticising others. "Teach us to number our days," says the psalm, "that we may get a heart of wisdom." But any day on which you have done some good to someone has not been wasted.
- You will find much in life to distress you. People can be careless, cruel, thoughtless, offensive, arrogant, harsh, destructive, insensitive, and rude. That is their problem, not yours. Your problem is how to respond. "No

one," a wise lady once said, "can make you feel inferior without your permission." The same applies to other negative emotions. Don't react. Don't respond. Don't feel angry, or if you do, pause for as long as it takes for the anger to dissipate, and then carry on with the rest of life. Don't hand others a victory over your own emotional state. Forgive, or if you can't forgive, ignore.

- If you tried and failed, don't feel bad. God forgives our failures as soon as we acknowledge them as failures – and that spares us from the self-deception of trying to see them as successes. No one worth admiring ever succeeded without many failures on the way. The great poets wrote bad poems, the great artists painted undistinguished canvases; not every symphony by Mozart is a masterpiece. If you lack the courage to fail, then you lack the courage to succeed.
- Always seek out the friendship of those who are strong where you are weak. None of us has all the virtues. Even a Moses needed an Aaron. The work of a team, a partnership, a collaboration with others who have different gifts or different ways of looking at things, is always greater than any one individual can achieve alone.
- Create moments of silence in your soul if you want to hear the voice of God.
- If something is wrong, don't blame others. Ask, how can I help to put it right?
- Always remember that you create the atmosphere that surrounds you. If you want others to smile, you must smile. If you want others to give, you must give. If

you want others to respect you, you must show your respect for them. How the world treats us is a mirror of how we treat the world.

- Be patient. Sometimes the world is slower than you are. Wait for it to catch up with you, for if you are on the right path, eventually it will.
- Never have your ear so close to the ground that you can't hear what an upright person is saying.
- Never worry when people say that you are being too idealistic. It is only idealistic people who change the world, and do you really want, in the course of your life, to leave the world unchanged?
- Be straight, be honest, and always do what you say you are going to do. There really is no other way to live.

LETTER 7:
Living Jewishly

IN MY LAST LETTER I spoke about some of the things I learned from Judaism about life. In this, I want to share some of the things I have learned from life about Judaism.

- Never ever be embarrassed about being a Jew. Our people has survived so long and contributed so much that you should see being Jewish as an honour and a responsibility.
- Some people look down on Jews; they always have. In which case, we have to walk tall, so that to see our face, they are forced to look up.
- Never compromise your principles because of others. Don't compromise on *kashrut* or any other Jewish practice because you happen to find yourself among non-Jews or non-religious Jews. *Non-Jews respect Jews who respect Judaism. They are embarrassed by Jews who are embarrassed by Judaism.*

- Never look down on others. Never think that being Jewish means looking down on gentiles. It doesn't. Never think that being a religious Jew entitles you to look down on non-religious Jews. It doesn't. The greatest Jew, Moses, was also, according to the Torah, "the humblest person on the face of the earth." Humility does not mean self-abasement. True humility is the ability to see good in others without worrying about yourself.
- Never stop learning. I once met a woman who was 103 and yet still seemed youthful. What, I asked her, was her secret? She replied, "Never be afraid to learn something new." Then I realised that learning is the true test of age. If you are willing to learn, you can be 103 and still young. If you aren't, you can be 23 and already old.
- Never confuse righteousness with self-righteousness. They sound similar, but they are opposites. The righteous see the good in people; the self-righteous see the bad. The righteous make you feel bigger; the self-righteous make you feel small. The righteous praise; the self-righteous criticise. The righteous are generous; the self-righteous, grudging and judgmental. Once you know the difference, keep far from the self-righteous, who come in all forms, right and left, religious and secular. Win the respect of people you respect, and ignore the rest.
- Whenever you do a mitzva, stop and be mindful. Every mitzva is there to teach us something, and it makes all the difference to pause and remember why. Mindless Judaism is not good for the soul.

- When you *daven,* reflect carefully on the meaning of the words. Remember too that in davening we are part of a four-thousand-year-old choral symphony, made up of the voices of all the Jews of all the countries in all the centuries who said these words. Some said these prayers in the midst of suffering; others as they faced exile and expulsion; some even said them in the concentration camps. They are words sanctified by tears, but now we are saying them in the midst of freedom. The prayers of our ancestors have come true for us. Therefore our prayers honour them as well as God, for without them we would not today be Jews, and without us carrying on their tradition, their hopes would have been in vain.
- Don't worry if you can't keep up with the congregation. One word said from the heart is greater than a hundred said without understanding or attention.
- Always be willing to share your Judaism. On Shabbat or the festivals, invite guests into your home. Once a week, learn with people who know less than you. The difference between material and spiritual goods is this: With material things – like wealth or power – the more you share, the less you have. With spiritual things – like knowledge or friendship or celebration – the more you share, the more you have.
- Never be impatient with the details of Jewish life. *God lives in the details.* Judaism is about the poetry of the ordinary, the things we would otherwise take for granted. Jewish law is the sacred choreography of everyday life.

- God lives in the space we make for Him. Every mitzva we do, every prayer we say, every act of learning we undertake, is a way of making space for God.

LETTER 8:
Faith

SARA, DAVID, these are difficult times, times of risk and danger, recession and uncertainty. Don't think I am being naïve if I say: These are the times when we need faith. Not blind faith, naïve optimism, but the kind of faith that says we are not helpless and we are not alone.

The Jewish people have been around for longer than almost any other. We have known our share of suffering. And still we are here, still young, still full of energy, still able to rejoice and celebrate and sing. Jews have walked more often than most through the valley of the shadow of death, yet they lost neither their humour nor their hope.

Faith is not certainty; it is the courage to live with uncertainty. Faith does not mean seeing the world as you would like it to be; it means seeing the world exactly as it is, yet never giving up the hope that we can make it better by the way we live – by acts of *ḥen* and *ḥesed,* graciousness and kindness, and by forgiveness and generosity of spirit.

In Judaism, faith does not mean "believing six impossible things before breakfast" (*Alice in Wonderland*). No faith respects human intelligence more. Jews argue: we take nothing for granted. We say, "The Lord is my shepherd," yet no Jew is a sheep. We are commanded to teach our children to ask questions. Ours is a questioning religion. What then is faith?

Faith is the knowledge that we are here for a reason, and that in our journey through life God is with us, lifting us when we fall, forgiving us when we fail, believing in us more than we believe in ourselves. This is not wishful thinking. It is a fact. But it is not a simple fact.

Just as we have to train ourselves to listen to great music or appreciate great art, so we have to train ourselves to sense the presence of God in our lives. That training comes in two forms. One is Torah, the other is mitzvot. Through Torah we learn what God asks of us. Through mitzvot, we practise doing God's will. That is how we open ourselves to God. Faith allows us to take risks and face the future without fear.

Sometimes we think that matters of the spirit are insubstantial compared to the battles of the real world. But consider this: The financial collapse of 2007–2008 came about because of a loss of *confidence* in institutions. Banks stopped lending because of a breakdown in *trust* in the ability of borrowers to repay. Trust and confidence are spiritual things, yet the market depends on them. The word "credit" comes from the Latin *credo,* which means *Ani maamin,* "I believe."

After an earlier great crash, Franklin D. Roosevelt famously said, "The only thing we have to fear is fear itself." Faith defeats fear, and gives us the confidence to survive every loss and begin again. Don't believe that faith is a small thing. It isn't. Whatever else you do in the coming year, practise your faith and renew it daily. The Jewish people kept faith alive. Faith kept the Jewish people alive.

So what do you do if, God forbid, you find yourself in the midst of crisis? You lose your job. You miss the promotion you were expecting. You find yourself with a medical condition that requires a major change of lifestyle. You make a bad investment decision that costs you dearly. You find an important relationship in your life under stress. Any of the thousand natural shocks that flesh is heir to can plunge you without warning into crisis. How do you survive the trauma and the pain?

There's one biblical passage that's deeply helpful. It's the famous, enigmatic story in Genesis 32 in which, at night, Jacob wrestles with an unknown, unnamed adversary: "Jacob was left alone, and a man wrestled with him till daybreak." It was this passage that gave the Jewish people their name, Israel, meaning "One who struggles with God and with man and prevails." The key phrase is when Jacob says to the stranger, "I will not let you go until you bless me." *Within every crisis lies the possibility of blessing*. Events that at the time were the most painful are also those that in retrospect we see most made us grow.

Crisis forces us to make difficult but necessary decisions. It makes us ask, "Who am I and what really matters to me?" It plunges us from the surface to the depths, where we discover strengths we didn't know we had, and a clarity of purpose we had hitherto lacked. So you have to say to every crisis, "I will not let you go until you bless me."

The struggle isn't easy. Though Jacob was undefeated, he "limped." Battles leave scars. Yet God is with us even when He seems to be against us. For if we refuse to let go of Him, He refuses to let go of us, giving us the strength to survive and emerge stronger, wiser, blessed.

The oldest question in religion is: "Why do bad things happen to good people?" But there are two ways of asking this question. The first is, "Why has God done this to me?" Never ask this question, because we will never know the answer. God cares for us, but He also cares for everyone and everything. We think of now; God thinks of eternity. We could never see the universe from God's point of view. So we will never find the answer to the question "Why me?"

But there is another way of asking the question. "Given that this has happened, what does God want me to learn from it? How is He challenging me to grow? How is He calling on me to respond?" Asking it this way involves looking forward, not back. "Why did God do this?" is the wrong question. The right one is: "How shall I live my life differently because this has happened?"

That is how to deal with crisis. Wrestle with it, refusing to let it go until it blesses you, until you emerge stronger, better, or wiser than you were before. *To be a Jew is not to accept defeat.* That is the meaning of faith.

LETTER 9:
Making a Blessing over Life

SARA, DAVID, Yom Kippur is the day on which we give a reckoning of our life, remembering how short life is, and how important it is, therefore, to live it well. "Teach us to number our days," says the psalm, "that we may get a heart of wisdom."

What we know we can lose, we learn to cherish. That's why the Jewish people at the dawn of its history suffered slavery so that ever after they would value freedom and fight for it. It's why Abraham had to come almost to the point of losing his child, so that Jews would love and cherish children. Those lessons were so deep – burned into our collective unconscious – that they've lasted for thousands of years.

It's no small thing that on the holiest day of the Jewish year *we think about the possibility of death, so that for the rest of the year we will love life.* Jews are the people who more than any other see God in life – this life, down here on earth.

Many other religions didn't do this. They thought that God was to be found in life after death, or in a monastic retreat, or in mystical ecstasy. For them the holy was *somewhere else*. For us the holy is in the here and now. The Jewish toast is *Leḥayim,* "To life." Moses' great command was *Uvaḥarta baḥayim,* "Choose life." From Rosh HaShana to Yom Kippur we pray: "Remember us for life, King who delights in life, and write us in the Book of Life for Your sake, God of life."

To find God you don't need to climb mountains, cross oceans, or travel to a fabled land. God is in the breath we breathe, the acts we do, the prayers we say, the love we give. God, vaster than the universe, is closer to us than we are to ourselves. Our first prayer every morning is *Modeh Ani,* "I thank You, living and eternal King, who has restored my soul in mercy." Thank You, God, for giving me back my life.

The whole of Judaism is a sustained discipline in *not taking life for granted*: the thanks we say in our prayers, the blessings we make over every pleasure, the way *kashrut* turns eating into a holy act and the laws of Jewish family life sanctify the act of love. Shabbat stops us from travelling through life so fast that we never get to enjoy the view.

The financial crash of 2007–2008 should teach us something. You can invest in the stock exchange, but the market can crash. You can invest in a house but prices can fall. You can follow secular trends but they can deceive and disappoint and leave you counting the cost. The best investment is in a life well lived, a life of meaning and principle and purpose, if possible framed by a happy marriage, a warm and embracing family, and a strong and supportive community.

Judaism helps us find these things. It sanctifies our families and homes. It gives us values to share with our children. As a way of life, it's been tested for longer than any other. As a source of wisdom, it is unparalleled in its depth and breadth. Judaism gives us roots to keep us grounded and wings to help us fly. Mitzvot train us in healthful habits of the heart. Prayer is the renewable energy of the soul, and faith is its satellite navigation system. Every blessing we make is a way of saying "Yes" to life. God is the God of life and Judaism is the religion of life.

Throughout history the pendulum has swung between two kinds of society: puritanical cultures that distrust pleasure, and hedonistic cultures that worship it. We do something better than either: we *sanctify* pleasure, taking our most physical drives and dedicating them to God. There are many faiths throughout the world, but none that has led a tiny people for so long, so profoundly, to find joy in life.

And yes, life can be hard and full of the possibility of loss, pain, disappointment, and grief. But the solution is not to avoid taking risks. It is to cultivate the things that give us strength: the love of family and friends, the support of a community, the habit of prayer that allows us to lean on God, and the faith that God has faith in us, forgiving our faults and giving us the strength, after every failure, to begin again. Judaism was the first religion in history to place love at the heart of the spiritual life: Love the Lord your God with all your heart, all your soul, and all your might. Love your neighbour. Love the stranger. The greatest love song in all religious literature is *Shir HaShirim*, the Song of Songs.

And what we love most – because that is where God is to be found – is life itself. That is our greatest strength. It enabled our ancestors to survive every persecution. It helped Holocaust survivors to survive. It gave the Jewish people the courage to rebuild the Land and State of Israel. That's why our greatest prayer on this day of days is: "Write us in the Book of Life." We don't ask for wealth or fame, stardom or success. We don't pray to be spared trials and tribulations. We just ask for life.

That is what Judaism is: a life of love and a love of life. All the rest is commentary.

LETTER 10: Finding Happiness

SARA, DAVID, not everything in the coming year will be under our control. It never is. "On Rosh HaShana it is written and on Yom Kippur it is sealed." The book is being written now but we don't get to read it in advance. Even in the twenty-first century, when human beings have decoded the genome and photographed the birth of galaxies, there is one thing not even the greatest Nobel Prize–winning scientist knows: what tomorrow will bring. We live with uncertainty. That is the human condition and always will be.

But what matters *will* be under our control. How will we act and react? Will we behave honourably, graciously, generously? Will we help others? Will we make sacrifices for the sake of our ideals? Will we live for something bigger than the self? Will we honour, praise, respect, admire? Will we give hospitality to the lonely, comfort to the bereaved, and support to those in need? Will we give our family time?

Will we give our soul the space to breathe? Will we love and thank God? Will we enhance other people's lives?

These are the questions we should ask ourselves on Yom Kippur. For it is not what happens to us on which our happiness depends. It depends on *how we respond* to what happens to us. So in this, my last letter to you before Yom Kippur, let me share with you ten secrets I've learned from Judaism. They will bring you happiness whatever fate has in store for you in the coming year.

1. *Give thanks*. Once a day, at the beginning of the morning prayers, thank God for all He has given you. This alone will bring you halfway to happiness. We already have most of the ingredients of a happy life. It's just that we tend to take these for granted and concentrate instead on our unfulfilled desires. Giving thanks in prayer focuses attention on the good and helps us keep a sense of proportion about the rest. It's better than shopping – and cheaper too.

2. *Praise*. Catch someone doing something right and say so. Most people, most of the time, are unappreciated. Being recognised, thanked, and congratulated by someone else is one of the most empowering things that can happen to us. So don't wait for someone to do it for you: do it for someone else. You will make their day, and that will help make yours. *Aleinu leshabe'aḥ* means "It's our duty to praise."

3. *Spend time with your family.* Keep Shabbat, so that there is at least one time a week when you sit down to have a meal together with no distractions – no television, no phone, no email, just being together, talking together, celebrating one another's company. Happy marriages and families need dedicated time.

4. *Discover meaning.* Take time, once in a while, to ask the Yom Kippur questions, "Why am I here? What do I hope to achieve? How best can I use my gifts? What would I wish to be said about me when I am no longer here?" Finding meaning is essential to a fulfilled life – and how will you find it if you never look? If you don't know where you want to be, you will never get there however fast you run.

5. *Live your values.* Most of us believe in high ideals, but we act on them only sporadically. The best thing to do is to establish habits that get us to enact those ideals daily. That is what mitzvot are: ideals in action, constantly rehearsed.

6. *Forgive.* This is the emotional equivalent of losing excess weight. Life is too short to bear a grudge or seek revenge. Forgiving someone is good for them but even better for you. The bad has happened. It won't be made better by your dwelling on it. Let it go. Move on.

7. *Keep growing.* Don't stand still, especially in the life of the spirit. The Jewish way to change the world is

to start with yourself. Anne Frank once wrote: "How wonderful it is that nobody need wait a single moment before starting to improve the world."

8. *Learn to listen.* Often in conversation we spend half our time thinking of what we want to say next instead of paying attention to what the other person is saying. Listening is one of the greatest gifts we can give to someone else. It means that we are open to them, that we take them seriously, that we accept graciously their gift of words. The keyword in Judaism is *Shema,* which simply means "Listen."

9. *Create moments of silence in the soul.* Liberate yourself, if only five minutes daily, from the tyranny of technology, the phone, the laptop, and all the other electronic intruders. Remember that God is in every breath we breathe. Inhale the heady air of existence, and feel the joy of being.

10. *Transform suffering.* When bad things happen to you, use them to sensitise you to the pain of others. The people who survived tragedy and became stronger as a result did not ask, "Who did this to me?" They asked, "What does this allow me to do that I could not have done before?" They didn't curse the darkness; instead they lit a candle. They refused to become victims of circumstance. They became, instead, agents of hope.

Life's too full of blessings to waste time and attention on artificial substitutes. Live, give, forgive, celebrate, and praise. These are still the best ways of making a blessing over life, thereby turning life into a blessing.

Sara, David, our beloved children: You will never know how many blessings you have given your mother and me. The best we can give you is to pray that God help you to be a blessing to others. Be the best you can, be an ambassador for Judaism and the Jewish people, use each day to do something demanding, and never be afraid to learn and grow.

We love you. May God write you and your children in the Book of Life.

INTRODUCTION TO LETTERS TO THE NEXT GENERATION 2

Yom Kippur, the Jewish day of days, is a time when we do more than confess and seek atonement for our sins. It's the supreme day of *teshuva,* which means "returning, coming home." To come home we have to ask who we are and where we truly belong. It is a day when we reaffirm our identity.

There were times when this was high drama. Periodically, from Visigoth Spain in the seventh century to Spain and Portugal in the fifteenth, Jews were confronted with the choice: convert or be expelled. Sometimes it was: convert or die. Most did not convert but some did. They were known in Hebrew as *anusim* (people who acted under pressure), and in Spanish as conversos or (as a term of abuse) Marranos.

Outwardly they behaved as if they were Christians or Muslims but secretly they kept their faith as Jews.

Once a year, at great risk, they would make their way to the synagogue as their way of saying, "A Jew I am and a Jew I will remain." This may explain the prayer before *Kol Nidrei*, giving permission to pray with "transgressors" (*avaryanim*). It may also be why *Kol Nidrei* became so deeply engraved in the Jewish heart, because of the tears of those who asked God to forgive them for vows they had taken through fear of death. On Yom Kippur even the most estranged Jew came home.

Today, thankfully, Jews are under no such threat. But being Jewish hasn't always been easy in the contemporary world, not just because of antisemitism and attacks on Israel but also because the whole thrust of our culture has little time for religious faith. So I have written this little book hoping it will help you answer some of the questions you may be asking as you reflect on how you will live in the year to come. I've written it in the form of letters to two Jewish students. They aren't actual people, but their questions are those I'm most often asked.

Writing it, I've held in mind the memory of four very special people: the late Susi and Fred Bradfield, whose lives were a sustained tutorial in Jewish commitment and generosity; the late Marc Weinberg, one of the leaders of his generation, who died in Israel last year at the age of 35; and my late mother, Libby, who died on the first night of Sukkot 5771, to whom I and my brothers owe so much. May their memories be a blessing.

May God be with you and the Jewish people in the coming year. May He forgive us our failings, heed our prayers, and write us in the Book of Life.

Jonathan Sacks
Tishrei 5772

LETTER 1:
A Belated Reply

DEAR RUTH, DEAR MICHAEL, you've been writing to me from time to time over the past year and somehow I was always too busy to reply. But now, as the Holy Days are approaching, I feel guilty at not having taken the time. So, belatedly, I'm writing back.

I don't know if you know one another, but I know that you are both at university, both thinking about what lies ahead: for you, for Jews, for humanity. From your letters and many others I receive, I know that you are both concerned about the hostility to Israel on campus. You fear a return of antisemitism. You wonder what the future holds for Israel and for Jews.

You have deep questions about religion in general and Judaism in particular. Does faith make sense? Aren't the new atheists right? Isn't religion based on ideas that have been disproved or at least overtaken by science? Can we really believe in a God who cares for us when He doesn't prevent a 9/11 or the Japanese earthquake? Can we believe in the Jewish God after the Holocaust?

As for Judaism: Yes, it may have given humanity world-changing ideas. But the world now has those ideas. Do we really need to stay different, distinctive, set apart? Isn't Judaism simply irrelevant to the twenty-first century?

Besides which, you tell me you are underwhelmed by what you experience of Jewish life. You find synagogue services boring. The rituals of Judaism leave you unmoved and perplexed. If Pesaḥ is about freedom, Shabbat about rest, Yom Kippur about feeling sorry for the wrong we do, why so many laws? Why not just focus on the essentials?

You put it very well, Ruth. You said that Judaism sometimes seems to you like one of those large packages that arrives in the post. You open it and find that most of it is foam wrapping and the object inside is actually very small. Why does Judaism need to surround itself with so much protective packaging?

I will try to answer these questions as best I can, though time is short, yours and mine. But first I want to try to answer the question you haven't asked but which I feel is there, just below the surface. For what you are really asking is: Why be Jewish? Why stay Jewish? Why live a Jewish life? How does it help you be the person you want to be?

Why when the pressures are so great, of finding a job, keeping a job, handling all the demands on your time, spend that time on a faith you find difficult and a way of life you find uninspiring? Why bother? That is the first question. From it all else follows. Tomorrow I will try to write you an answer.

LETTER 2:
A Historian's Honour

DEAR RUTH, DEAR MICHAEL, I said yesterday that I would try to give you an answer to the question why stay Jewish. There are many answers, and to understand them is the work of a lifetime. But we have to start somewhere, and probably the more unexpected the starting point, the better.

Like you I studied at university, so I knew vaguely about an eccentric Oxford don, a historian and a writer about English literature. He was a Fellow of All Souls, which meant that he was one of the brightest minds of his generation.

His name was A. L. Rowse and he was best known for his theory about the identity of the "dark lady" of Shakespeare's sonnets. He died in 1997, and shortly before that, in 1995, he published a book called *Historians I Have Known*. I was reading it one day and I came to the last page.

There – it was the penultimate sentence of the book – I came across a remark that left me open-mouthed with amazement. Nothing had prepared me for it. A. L. Rowse was not Jewish, and as far as I know he had no connection with Jews other than those he knew at university.

This is what he wrote. "If there is any honour in all the world that I should like, it would be to be an honorary Jewish citizen." What an extraordinary remark from a wise man nearing the end of his life, reflecting on all that life, especially history, had taught him.

The British know about honours. So I could understand an Oxford don who had written over a hundred books admitting that a medal, an award, a knighthood would not go amiss. But "to be an honorary Jewish citizen" and to count that not just as an honour, but the *one above all* he would like to have – that was an extraordinary thing to say.

Why did he say it? I never met him. I did not know anyone who had. And by the time I read the book he was no longer alive. So I can only speculate.

Was it that Jews more than any other people in history cared about learning, education, and the life of the mind? That they had contributed, vastly out of proportion to their numbers, many of the greatest intellects of the modern world? Was it that they were the first monotheists, the first to believe in a God who transcended the universe, creating it in forgiveness and love, making humanity in His image and endowing us with a dignity no other faith has ever equalled?

Was it that they had survived for so long – twice as long as Christianity, three times as long as Islam – and under some of the most adverse conditions ever experienced by a people? Was it, given that Rowse was a historian, the fact that

Jews were the first historians, the first to see God in history, the first even to think in terms of history?

Was it, given that he was a writer on literature, the fact that the Hebrew Bible is the greatest work of literature ever written? Was it the vision of Moses, the poetry of psalms, the social conscience of Amos, the hope of Isaiah, the wisdom of Ecclesiastes, the passion of the Song of Songs? Or that Jews had given humanity its most basic moral concepts: free will, responsibility, justice and the rule of law, *ḥesed* and the rule of compassion, *tzedaka* and the principle of equity?

Who knows? But I know this – that if they offered to make you a dame, Ruth, or a knight, Michael, you wouldn't refuse. You wouldn't consider it trivial or irrelevant. But if Rowse was right, it turns out that you have already been given an honour greater than these. Don't forget it or give it away.

LETTER 3: Great Expectations

Dear Rabbi, could you explain this a little more fully? Being Jewish doesn't feel like an honour to me.

Yours, Ruth

RUTH, sometimes we lack perspective. Think of sitting in a car in a traffic jam. Your view of the road ahead is obscured by the car in front. Now think of how the scene would seem different if you were in an airplane looking down. You could see not just the road but the whole vast landscape. Caught in the thick of Jewish life, down here on the ground so to speak, we do not always see its beauty, its grandeur, its spiritual passion and moral power.

I gave the example yesterday of A. L. Rowse. On another occasion I was reading a book about inflation by the economist and former editor of *The Times,* William Rees-Mogg, when – again with no obvious connection to the subject at hand – I came across this sentence: "One of the gifts of Jewish culture to Christianity is that it has taught Christians to think like Jews. Any modern man who has not learned to think as though he were a Jew can hardly be said to have learned to think at all." Nietzsche, not normally thought of as a philosemite, wrote: "Wherever Jews have won influence they have taught men to make finer distinctions, more rigorous inferences, and to write in a more luminous and cleanly fashion."

Winston Churchill said: "Some people like the Jews, and some do not. But no thoughtful man can deny the fact that they are beyond question the most formidable and the most remarkable race which has ever appeared in the world."

These people were telling us something from a distance that we – sitting in our metaphorical traffic jam – don't always see. We see the road but not the landscape, the car in front of us but not the open space half a mile ahead.

Judaism really was world changing. Two other religions – Christianity and Islam – borrowed from it and became the faith of more than half the seven billion people alive today. A huge proportion of shapers of the modern mind were Jewish at least by lineage, from Marx, Freud, and Einstein to Sergey Brin of Google and Mark Zuckerberg of Facebook.

Judaism has been like a sun sending out rays in all directions while remaining in itself the source. Why? What was the source of its power? And what does that have to do with us, with you and me, here, now?

The answer, I think, is that we tend to become what we believe. Experiments have repeatedly shown that when teachers have high expectations of their students, the students go on to do well. When they have low expectations, the students do badly.

No religion, no culture, no civilisation has ever had higher expectations of the human person than Judaism – and that applies to you and me.

We are each, says the Torah, created in the image and likeness of God, gifted with the freedom and blessed by the intellect He has given us. One life, said the Sages, is like a universe. Destroy a life and you destroy a universe. Save a life and you save a universe. We are called on to be, says the Talmud, God's partners in the work of creation. Every individual, says Maimonides, should see him- or herself and the world as evenly poised between good and evil, so that our next act may tilt the balance of our life and the very fate of life itself.

Though some of these ideas were later borrowed by others – by Christianity, Islam, even secular philosophy – no group has ever believed them so deeply or lived out their implications so consistently.

Jews have had an influence out of all proportion to their numbers, because they believed in the individual and his or her power to change the world for the better. Believing that God had high expectations of them, they did great things.

If I had the choice of all *the cultures in the world, I would still choose the one that had the highest expectations of what an individual can achieve in a lifetime.* That is why I consider it an honour to be a Jew.

LETTER 4:
The Pursuit of Happiness

Dear Rabbi, I read your reply to Ruth, but how would that actually make a difference to my life? Why should I live differently in the future because of the way Jews lived in the past?
Michael

MICHAEL, you are about to begin your journey into the wide world of earning a living and making a life. When making your choices, remember this: *We are as big as the ideals by which we live.* We have only one life to live, so we had better choose those ideals carefully. And the ideals on offer in today's culture are very small indeed – not all but most.

What a strange world it is in which we value people by what they earn or what they own, the clothes they wear, the cars they drive, the houses they live in, and the holidays they take. These things are not unimportant. One great rabbi, the third-century Sage known as Rav, said, "In the World to

Come we will have to give an account of every legitimate pleasure we denied ourselves in this life." Judaism is as unpuritanical a religion as it is possible to be.

But this is the gift-wrapping of life, not life itself. I studied philosophy at university, but the deepest philosophy lessons I ever learned came from attending Jewish funerals. That's when we face the truth about what makes a life worthwhile. We catch a glimpse of what lives on after us, what people will remember us for, what difference we make in this brief span of years that is all God gives us.

No one ever delivered a *hesped,* a funeral oration, saying: "Mr. X. What a man he was. He drove a Lamborghini, dressed in Armani, wore a Patek-Philippe, had a villa in Cap Ferrat and a pied-a-terre in Mayfair. This was a giant. We shall not see his like again." We know that a speech like that would be mad.

Let me let you into a secret. There are good reasons why the world wants us to live our lives for the wrong reasons. If no one worried what they wore, if all they cared about in a car was whether it gets you from A to B, if they ate simple food that just happens to be good for you, if they were more interested in serving others than having others at great expense serve them, economists would panic.

We would be healthier and happier, there would be less envy, competition, and strife, and we would work less hard with less stress and more time to enjoy life. Meanwhile, advertisers would be out of a job, manufacturers would suffer a slump in demand, businesspeople would warn of the risk of recession, and retailers would tell shareholders of lower profits and reduced dividends. So, for the sake of the greatest happiness of the greatest number, we make ourselves unhappy.

Somewhere in our souls, Michael, we have to create space for a voice of sanity that is so easy to miss among the emails and texts and tweets, the noise and bustle and relentless pressure that is making slaves of us all while telling us that we are the most fortunate generation that ever lived, having witnessed Steve Jobs descending the mountain, holding in his hands the two tablets, iPad 1 and iPad 2, on which are written the sacred words that you can download in less than a minute and read in a choice of fonts.

We have to make space for the things that really matter: relationships, marriage, the family, being part of a community, celebrating, giving thanks, being part of a tradition and its wisdom, a faith and its blessings, giving to others and sharing with them our joys and grief.

There has to be room in life for something bigger than us, larger than self-interest and longer than a lifetime. There are times when we have to let the soul sing, to express gratitude and know that what we have is God's gift. That's what living Jewishly does. It structures our lives around the things that matter – the things that are important but not urgent, and therefore tend to be neglected until it is too late. Don't leave it too late.

For this is what Judaism shows us: how to take hold of life with both hands and make a blessing over it. That is what distinguishes happiness from mere pleasure, and gives meaning to our years and days.

LETTER 5:
A Life That Matters

Can you give me an example of what you mean by making a blessing over life?

Yours, Ruth

DID YOU EVER HEAR the story, Ruth, about Alfred Nobel, the man who created the prizes that bear his name? In 1888, Nobel, the man who invented dynamite, was reading his morning papers when, with a shock, he found himself reading his own obituary. It turned out that a journalist had made a simple mistake. It was Nobel's *brother* who had died. What horrified Nobel was what he read. It spoke about "the dynamite king" who had made a fortune from explosives. Nobel suddenly realised that if he didn't change his life, that was all he would be remembered for. At that moment he decided to dedicate his fortune to creating five annual prizes for those who'd made outstanding contributions in physics, chemistry, medicine, literature, and peace. Nobel chose to be remembered for peace.

What will we be remembered for? That is the question Judaism makes us confront, especially on Rosh HaShana and Yom Kippur. Let me tell you a true story, tragic but also deeply inspiring. It happened in the summer of 2010. A young man, Marc Weinberg, brilliant, gifted, with a devoted wife and two beautiful young children, had been diagnosed with leukaemia. For two and a half years, helped by advanced medical technology and lifted by the prayers of friends, he fought with all his strength against the civil war raging inside his body. In the end it was too much, and he died, still in his mid-thirties.

Marc was no ordinary young man. He was a person of the most profound religious belief and practice, who spent every spare moment of his crowded, short life helping others and bringing out the best in them. By the sheer force of his example he transformed lives. He taught people the power of possibility and helped them become better than they thought they were. Was this his reward? To die so young? Abraham once asked, "Shall the Judge of all the earth not do justice?" There are moments that can shake your faith to its foundations. Yet, as I stood at his funeral, this was not the feeling that swept over me. Instead I felt a strange, quite unexpected access of faith.

For around me, gathered at short notice, were more than a thousand mourners, many of them his age or younger. Through their tears I saw the difference he had made to their lives. He wasn't rich or famous. He had lived all too briefly. Yet each of them had a story to tell of how he had helped them, inspired them, befriended them when they were lonely, lifted them when they were suffering some personal crisis. Each of those blessings had given rise to others in turn, in a series of ever-widening ripples of good.

There is a film, *Pay It Forward,* in which the hero, a young schoolboy, is set an assignment by his social science teacher: "Come up with a practical plan to change the world and improve humankind." Moved by the plight of people he sees in difficulties – a homeless man, his alcoholic mother, his badly scarred teacher – he suddenly envisages a way. Normally, kindnesses are reciprocated. They are "paid *back.*" What if they were paid *forward*? What if we made it a condition of doing someone some good, that they agreed to do good to someone else in need? Could you not make virtue contagious, creating an epidemiology of generosity?

The film ends on a note of tragedy. The child dies. But the story is a tutorial in hope, because the child does succeed in changing lives in ways no one could have foreseen. That is what I felt among the crowd of mourners that day. We had come to honour the memory of one who, without ever saying so, taught people to pay it forward, and he had left behind him a vast legacy of blessings. And yes, he died young and left a tidal wave of grief. But he had also taught us how never to let grief, or suffering, or sadness have the last word. Before he died, he taught us how to live.

We wept that day. I believe God wept too. Shmuel Yosef Agnon, the Nobel Prize–winning writer, once speculated that *Kaddish,* the prayer for the dead, is our way of offering comfort to God for the loss of one of His children. Mortality is written into the human condition, but so too is the possibility of immortality, in the good we do that continues, long after we are here, to beget further good. There are lives that defeat death and redeem existence from tragedy. We knew, that day, that we had known one of them.

Ruth, Michael, none of us knows how long we will live. We just know that one day we will die. Life is too short to waste on "the small stuff." Judaism teaches us the simplest, deepest truth of all. You make a blessing over life by being a blessing to those whose lives you touch.

LETTER 6:
The Moral Voice

I can understand the difference Judaism makes at home, or in synagogue, or among friends, but how will it make a difference to the way I pursue my career?

Michael

BY HELPING YOU to do the right and the good, Michael. We've been shaken by scandals involving bankers, financiers, politicians and parliamentarians, journalists, and the police. They have acted in ways at worst immoral, at best irresponsible.

We now know we can't take morality for granted. Even people in positions of trust can betray that trust. We also know why. Not because they are evil, but because they have creative consciences: "If everyone else is doing it, why shouldn't I? Who will notice? Besides which, it's a brutal, competitive, beat-or-be-beaten world. And strictly speaking, it's legal. Even if it isn't, I can hire a lawyer who will argue it is. The gain is great, the downside small." That's how intelligent people come to do foolish things.

If you want to be protected against doing foolish things, be guided by a wisdom higher than your own and older than your contemporaries. When it comes to moral wisdom, there is no tradition stronger than Judaism.

The voice of Torah is the moral voice of Western civilisation. It says: Love your neighbour as yourself. It says: Love the stranger, for you were once strangers. It says: Justice, justice shall you pursue. It says: Act justly, love mercy, and walk humbly with your God.

Listen to these words from the *haftara* of Yom Kippur, taken from the book of Isaiah:

> Is this the kind of fast I have chosen, only a day for people to humble themselves? Is it only for bowing one's head like a reed and for lying in sackcloth and ashes? Is that what you call a fast, a day acceptable to the Lord?
>
> Is not this the kind of fasting I have chosen: to loose the chains of injustice and untie the cords of the yoke, to set the oppressed free and break every yoke? Is it not to share your food with the hungry and to provide the poor wanderer with shelter – when you see the naked, to clothe them, and not to turn away from your own flesh and blood?

Who else speaks this way, Michael? Not the Egyptians or Babylonians, the ancient Greeks or Romans, not Descartes or Kant or Nietzsche or Schopenhauer. Albert Einstein spoke about the "almost fanatical love of justice" that made him "thank his stars" that he belonged to the Jewish tradition. Jews added something, an inflection, an accent, an urgency and passion, to the moral voice of humankind.

Of course Jews don't have a monopoly on conscience or virtue. We don't claim to have. We believe, as Rabbeinu Nissim Gerondi (1180–1263) says in the introduction to his commentary on the Talmud, that the moral commands have been binding since the first humans set foot on earth. Humans, as evolutionary psychologists have been proving, have a moral sense. It's what makes us social animals.

But let me be blunt. Whatever you choose to do, there will be times when you will be tempted – to cut corners, take advantage of your situation, bend the rules to your own advantage, use privileged access or insider information, or do something you know you should not do but which other people seem to be getting away with. There is no life without temptation.

That is when all the habits of the heart that Judaism inculcates make a difference: the prayers we say, the Torah we learned, the stories we heard as children, the standards we know are expected of us, even the mere knowledge that, though no one else may know what we are doing, God knows, and God is the voice of conscience in the human heart.

This matters more than I can say. When I think of the people who had such gifts, such talents, such promising careers, who were so well thought of – and then, because of a moment's temptation, the prospect of a quick profit, an easy gain, they put it all at risk – then I thank God for whispering the word that is always the hardest to hear: the word "no."

Ruth, Michael, believe me: If the only thing Judaism does for us in a lifetime is to keep us from temptation, it would still be worth all the money in the world.

LETTER 7:
The Greatness of Smallness

But why me, Rabbi? There are other Jews. They will keep the tradition going. Why me?

Ruth

RUTH, I know the difficulties you feel, the challenges you face, the problems you find in Jewish life today. We can talk about these in the days ahead. But I would not have done my duty had I not made it as clear as I can that we need you and the world needs us.

There are not many Jews in the world today. We represent less than a fifth of a percent of the population of the world. For every Jew alive today there are a hundred Muslims and 183 Christians. We are a tiny people. We always were. Moses said so, thirty-three hundred years ago. "Not because you are numerous did God love you or choose you, because you are the smallest of all nations" (Deut. 7:7).

I've often wondered about this. Why are we so small? One reason, of course, is the history of Jewish persecution, of which the Holocaust was the greatest but by no means the only tragedy. Many Jews died because of their faith.

Another reason, and a good one, is that we never sought to convert the world. Had we done so, there would be more Jews. But we believed, and still do, that you don't have to be Jewish to encounter God or get to heaven. That is one of Judaism's most beautiful beliefs. In this global age with its multi-faith societies, the sooner we recognise the integrity of other sources of wisdom and virtue the better.

But there's a third reason, and it's hinted at in a strange story in the eighth chapter of the book of Judges. It's set more than three thousand years ago, in the days before there was a king in Israel. God tells Gideon, the charismatic Jewish leader at the time, to go and fight the Midianites, who have been attacking Israel.

Gideon assembles an army of 32,000 soldiers. "Too many," says God. "Tell everyone who wants to, to go home." Some 22,000 do so. Now he has only 10,000 men. "Still too many," says God. He tells Gideon to take them to the river, see how they drink water, and send home all those who bend down to drink. Some 9,700 do so, and he sends them home. Now there are only 300 left, a ridiculously small number with which to fight a war. "Now go and fight," he tells Gideon. They do, and they win. Somewhere in that story lies the secret of Jewish smallness.

Through the story of the Jews, God is telling the world that a nation need not be big to be great. Small groups can make a large difference. Which is why Jews have contributed to most fields of human endeavour out of all proportion to their numbers.

But that places an enormous responsibility on each of us. The future of Judaism is in our hands, Ruth, and to a people as small as ours, every life makes a significant difference. Every loss is a tragedy.

Don't leave. Don't give up. Don't abandon your faith, your people, your history, your heritage. Stay and contribute. Stay and argue. Stay and bring the Jewish world a little closer to what it ought to be. If it really is, as A. L. Rowse thought it was, an honour to be a Jew, wear that honour with pride and show it to be an honour by the way you live.

LETTER 8:
Faith

Dear Rabbi, I'll grant you all the beautiful things you say about Judaism. But aren't they all irrelevant? Judaism is a religion, and religion has been replaced by science. We don't need to believe in God anymore. When faith made sense, Judaism made sense. But now, it doesn't make sense at all.

Sincerely, Michael

DEAR MICHAEL, consider this: To explain the universe we no longer need Genesis; we have science. To control the universe we no longer need prayer; we have technology. To prevent the abuse of power we don't need prophets; we have elections. To achieve prosperity we don't need blessings; we have economists.

If we fall ill we don't go to a rabbi; we go to a doctor. If we feel guilty we no longer need confession; we can go to a psychotherapist. If we are depressed we no longer need the book of Psalms; we can take Prozac. And if we seek salvation we can go to a shopping centre, where we can buy happiness at a highly competitive price. So who needs religion?

Yet *religion survives.* Everywhere except in Europe, it's getting stronger. Today in the United States – still the world's leading economy – more people regularly attend a place of worship than they do in the theocratic state of Iran. In China, the world's fastest growing economy, there are more people in church on a Sunday than there are members of the Communist Party, and this in a place that, a half century ago, Chairman Mao Zedong declared "religion-free."

If religion has been declared dying, even dead, why is it still so vigorously alive? Because none of the institutions of the modern world – science, technology, liberal democracy, and the market economy – can answer the three great questions that every reflective human being must ask:

- Who am I?
- Why am I here?
- How then shall I live?

Science deals with causes, not purposes. It tells us how, not why. Technology gives us power but cannot tell us how to use that power. Liberal democracy gives us maximal space to live in accordance with our conscience but does not presume to be that conscience. The market gives us choices but does not tell us how to choose.

Yet we seek an answer to those questions, and that is not a minor fact about us. It is constitutive of our humanity. *Homo sapiens* is the meaning-seeking animal. That is why religion survives and always will. To put it as simply as possible: *Science takes things apart to see how they work. Religion puts things together to see what they mean*. These are different activities, and we need "the great partnership" of both. Judaism respects science, so much so that two thousand years ago the Sages coined a special blessing to be said "on seeing one of the sages of the nations of the world," meaning what we would nowadays call scientists. Moses Maimonides in the twelfth century said that science and metaphysics are ways of achieving the love and fear of God.

But science is only half the story. It can analyse the chemical composition of a great painting but it cannot tell us what makes it a great painting. It can tell us how our instinctual drives were formed but it cannot tell us which of those drives to yield to and which to resist. It can measure the cosmic microwave background radiation that in 1964 enabled American physicists Penzias and Wilson to prove that the universe had an origin in time. But it cannot tell us what existed before or exists beyond the universe.

Who are we? Why are we here? How then should we live? Those are the questions the answer for which we need faith, and they will continue to be asked as long are there are humans on earth. Faith is the answer to the questions that will remain even when all the science has been done.

LETTER 9:
The Dignity of Purpose

What makes you convinced that those questions have an answer? Perhaps life has no meaning. That's what the Greek philosopher Epicurus thought. It's what Bertrand Russell thought. It's what today's atheists think. The universe just exists. We just exist. There is no reason. Why should we think otherwise?

Michael

BECAUSE, Michael, humans have always lifted their eyes beyond the visible horizon. That is what led Columbus and Vasco da Gama to embark on their voyages of discovery. It's what led Newton to lay the foundations of science and Descartes to set out the agenda of modern philosophy. Humans – real humans who think – are never satisfied with the answer "It just is." Why does the universe exist? It just does. Why are we here? We just are. How then shall we live? As we choose. That isn't thought, Michael, but the premature termination of thought.

Nothing suggests that the universe suddenly sprang into being 13.7 billion years ago for no reason and at random. Scientists have shown that it is almost impossibly finely tuned for the emergence of life. The entire structure of the universe is determined by six mathematical constants which, had they varied by a billionth or trillionth of a degree, would have resulted in no universe at all. Had the force of gravity been slightly different, for example, the universe would either have expanded or imploded in such a way as to preclude the formation of stars or planets.

This does not prove that "in the beginning God created..." But the only other hypothesis that would explain how we came to be is that there is an infinite number of parallel universes, one of which – ours – just happened to be amenable to life. My view is that if one universe spontaneously coming into being is hard to understand, an infinity of self-igniting universes is even harder to understand.

Imagine this: There is an infinity of universes, only one of which has the precise parameters ours has, making it amenable to life. Within that one universe – ours – there are a hundred billion galaxies, each containing on average a hundred billion stars, yet ours is the only one known to us that gave rise to life. Within the three million species of life thus far known, only one – *Homo sapiens* – is capable of self-conscious thought, capable, that is, of asking the question "Why?" And only if there is a life form capable of asking the question "Why?" is something in the universe conscious that there is a universe. Am I to suppose that all this happened by accident? That it just happened, period?

No: The simplest and most elegant hypothesis is the one Judaism introduced into the world long ago, that the universe was created by the God of love and forgiveness, who brought us into being in love and forgiveness, commanding us to love and forgive others.

Who, then, am I? The image of God. Why am I here? To sanctify life. How then shall I live? By the principles and laws God has taught us.

The universe is not as ancient polytheists and today's atheists believe, a meaningless clash of primal forces, each indifferent to the fact that we exist. We and the universe are here because Someone wanted us to be – One who lifts us when we fall, forgives us when we fail, who gave us the very freedom that makes humanity distinct from every other life form known to us, and who invites us to become His partners in the work of creation.

It is this belief alone that rescues life from meaninglessness, nihilism, and despair. It is true that there are people who sincerely believe that life as a whole is meaningless. You mentioned some of them. Another was my doctoral supervisor, the late Sir Bernard Williams, one of the most brilliant men I ever met. And it is true that we cannot resolve the disagreement either way, by scientific evidence or logical proof.

But all the great truths of life are like that. You cannot prove that it is better to trust than to be perennially suspicious, or that it is worth taking the risk of love and the commitment of marriage, or that it makes sense to bring children into the world, or that you should be generous and forgiving, or that you should live by altruism rather than by narrow self-interest.

Some people are unmoved by any of these ideals, just as there are people who do not see any meaning in life beyond fleeting pleasures and the certainty of death. For that matter there are people who live without music or a sense of humour or hope. But surely we would agree that such lives are foreshortened, impoverished in some way.

The historian Paul Johnson once wrote: "No people has ever insisted more firmly than the Jews that history has a purpose and humanity a destiny." Jews, he says, "stand right at the centre of the perennial attempt to give human life the dignity of a purpose." That is the truth at the heart of our faith.

LETTER 10: A Nation of Iconoclasts

I was interested in what you wrote to Michael, but surely all monotheists believe what we believe. What makes Judaism different?

Yours, Ruth

GOOD QUESTION, Ruth. One answer was given by Jeremiah in a line we say on Rosh HaShana: "I remember the devotion of your youth, how as a bride you loved me and followed me through the wilderness, through an unsown land."

Jews were the people willing to travel towards the unknown. Judaism began with two epic journeys, one by Abraham and Sarah, the other in the days of Moses. And note that both journeys were in exactly the opposite direction to the one we would expect. Normally people travel towards centres of civilisation. Abraham and Moses travelled away from the greatest civilisations of their day. Jews are *akshanim,* obstinate, counter-cultural. If the rest of the world is going one way, Jews go the other. They take what American poet Robert Frost called "the road less travelled."

So when people worshipped power, Jews stood up for the powerless. When societies were rigidly hierarchal, Jews taught that we each have equal dignity. When 90 percent of Europe was illiterate, Jews built schools to ensure that each of their children had an education. When the vast majority of humanity lived in poverty, Jews practised the principle of *tzedaka,* the duty of those who have more than they need to share with those who have less.

Judaism is the counter-voice in the human conversation. To be a Jew is to be an iconoclast, challenging the taken-for-granted assumptions of our time, willing to break the idols of the age.

Jews pioneered time and again. To quote Paul Johnson again, to the Jews "we owe the idea of equality before the law, both Divine and human; of the sanctity of life and the dignity of the human person; of the individual conscience and so of personal redemption; of the collective conscience and so of social responsibility; of peace as an abstract ideal and love as the foundation of justice, and many other items which constitute the basic moral furniture of the human mind."

But the foundational discovery that led to all the others was the idea of a God not within nature but beyond it, a God therefore who could not be seen but could nonetheless be heard, a God who, transcending the physical universe, summons us to transcend the purely physical universe of human desires and reflexes that have, throughout the ages, led people to violence, cruelty, and injustice.

Jews were different. We still are. Unlike atheists, we believe that the universe, and human life, have a purpose. Unlike Christians and Muslims we believe that you don't have to belong to our religion to have a relationship with God or a place in heaven.

Judaism doesn't believe that humans are tainted by original sin. It is a religion of questions and arguments; we don't believe that the highest state is blind obedience, silencing the intellect God gave us when He made us in His image.

Unlike today's secularists, we don't believe that morality is relative, or that marriage is just one lifestyle choice among many, or that there can be rights without responsibilities. And unlike today's materialists, we don't believe that human beings are just accidental configurations of selfish genes, that our noblest thoughts are no more than electrical impulses in the brain, and that our dreams, hopes, visions, and aspirations are mere illusions and self-deceptions.

Jews were different. They still are different. Judaism is about the dignity of difference. Throughout history Jews were the only people who consistently refused to assimilate to the dominant culture or convert to the majority faith. Jews were often a minority to teach the world that God cares about the rights of minorities. And to teach all of us that the majority is not always right, nor is the conventional wisdom always wise. That has meant that we have often been disliked. People hate to see their prejudices disturbed. But the world needs its dissenting voices – and that, Ruth, is what we are.

LETTER 11: Faith After the Holocaust

But how can you really believe after the Holocaust, when Jews cried out and Heaven was silent? When one and a half million innocent children were murdered, merely because their grandparents were Jews? How can anyone believe in God after that?

Yours, Michael

MICHAEL, that is the question of questions. But the truth is that I have known many Holocaust survivors.

They have become my friends, my mentors. They are among the strongest and most life-affirming people I have ever met. How they survived, seeing what they saw, knowing what they know, I have no idea. Yet in all the years, not one of them ever asked me, "Where was God at Auschwitz?" Some undoubtedly lost their faith in those years, some kept it, and some regained it in the course of time. Some never did believe, not then, not now.

But the question "Where was God?" was not born in the Holocaust. It was born the day Cain, the first human child, killed his brother Abel. God warned Cain beforehand, but He did not stop him. Why not? The answer, and it is a tough answer, is that God does not stop people doing what they have chosen to do. Without that there would be no freedom. The universe would be a vast prison camp. God isn't like that. A large part of the Hebrew Bible is the story of God's disappointment at what we have done with the freedom He gave us. But He does not take it back.

Now let me be candid. The Holocaust creates, for me, a continuing crisis of faith which gets deeper the more I read about it. How, after Auschwitz, can any of us ever again have faith, not in God but – in humanity?

The Holocaust did not take place long ago and far away. It happened less than a century ago in the heart of post-religious, enlightened, rationalist Europe: in the land, nation, and culture that produced Goethe, Schiller, Mozart, Beethoven, Kant, and Hegel, that claimed to have reached a new peak in human civilisation.

Nor was it carried out by uneducated masses. More than a half of those who sat together at Wannsee in January 1942 and planned the "Final Solution," the extermination of all of Europe's eleven million Jews, carried the title "doctor." They were either medical doctors or had doctorates.

Heidegger, the greatest German philosopher of the twentieth century, was an enthusiastic member of the Nazi party, betrayed his Jewish colleagues and students, and never, after the war, expressed remorse for what he had done.

Scientists, lawyers, judges, doctors, and academics all played their part in the extermination of the Jews and almost none registered a protest.

Not one of the disciplines claiming to be expressive of the new humanism acted as a barrier to inhumanity. Science proved no protection: The racial antisemitism born in Germany in the late nineteenth century was based on two so-called sciences, social Darwinism and the "scientific study of race." The former argued that societies evolved the way species did, by the strong ruthlessly eliminating the weak. The latter, a mix of biology and anthropology, held that humans are divided into different races, each with its own ineliminable characteristics. Thus Blacks, Jews, and others are inferior species. We now know both were wrong, but in those days they were part of the scientific consensus.

Philosophy was no protection. At his trial, Adolf Eichmann proved himself to be a disciple of Kantian ethics. Indeed many of Europe's greatest philosophers, among them Voltaire, Fichte, Hegel, Schopenhauer, and Nietzsche, together with Kant himself, expressed sentiments that were blatantly antisemitic.

The arts were no protection. We know that a string quartet played classical music in Auschwitz-Birkenau as one and a quarter million men, women, and children were gassed, burned, and turned to ash. Civilisation failed to civilise. The humanities did not prevent inhumanity.

Even today some of the world's most famous atheists are intolerant, abrasive, insensitive to human dignity, incapable of listening to views opposed to their own – not necessarily people I would trust to create a world of freedom and compassion.

It is not easy to have faith after Auschwitz. The Klausenberger Rav, Rabbi Yekutiel Halberstam, who lived through several extermination camps, once said, "The real miracle is that we who survived the Holocaust still have faith. That, my friends, is the greatest miracle of all."

Job, in the book that bears his name, said, "Though He slay me, yet will I trust in Him." Faith does not mean that, whatever we do, things will turn out fine. The freedom God gave us includes among other things the freedom to destroy ourselves. Freedom honours our humanity only if accompanied by responsibility. Faith is God's call to responsibility. God does not save us from ourselves. God teaches us how to save ourselves from ourselves.

The way He did so was simple. He taught us, at the beginning of the Torah, the book that was His greatest gift to us, that every human being, regardless of colour, class, or creed, is in God's own image, after His own likeness. Meaning: life is sacred.

Sacred. That is a religious word. I do not know any secular word that has the same moral force, the same power to cut through all sophisticated rationalisations. After the Holocaust we need God more than ever. For there is no limit to the evil men may do when they no longer believe that anything is sacred.

LETTER 12: Sacred Discontent

BUT THERE'S MORE. Ruth, Michael, bear with me because I want to explain one of the most difficult, revolutionary ideas of Judaism – something still not well understood but which is absolutely fundamental to our view of the world.

Judaism is a religion of what one writer called "sacred discontent." There's an ancient midrash – a rabbinical commentary dating back some fifteen centuries. It is asking the question: What made Abraham begin his religious quest? The answer it gives is very strange indeed.

It says that he was like a man on a journey in some remote place when he sees in the distance a palace in flames. He asks, "Can the palace be without an owner?" While he is puzzling about this, he hears a voice coming from the burning building saying, "I am the owner of the palace." So Abraham heard God saying, "I am the owner of the world."

This is a haunting story. Let's figure out what it means. Abraham is saying, the palace must have an owner. Someone designed this building, and had it built. Palaces don't suddenly appear of their own accord. And the owner, or at least someone working for him, must be there now, because you don't abandon a palace or leave it unattended. In which case, why is it burning? Somebody should be putting out the flames.

I have never heard a more profound and unsettling account of the nature of the universe. We believe that it is like a palace. Someone designed it. Someone built it. Someone therefore owns it. As I wrote before, the more we understand of how finely tuned the universe is for the emergence of stars, planets, and life, the less likely it is that it simply appeared by spontaneous self-generation. Someone made the universe that gave rise to us.

In which case, why is there so much evil and suffering and injustice and cruelty and violence and terror and disease and needless death? The universe is a contradiction. On the one hand, order; on the other, chaos. On the one hand, the palace; on the other, the flames.

Abraham lived, and we live, with that contradiction. And as the midrash indicates, there is only one way out. God is calling us, as He called Abraham: "Help Me put out the flames."

Why can't God do it Himself? If He can create an entire universe, why can't He eliminate evil and suffering and disease without our help? Because some of the evil is because He gave humans free will, and He can't take away that freedom without taking away our humanity. And because only if there is deterioration and decay can there be a physical universe capable of giving rise to life at all.

We are the dust of exploded stars, so scientists tell us. So, without the explosions there would be no us. Without illness there would be no death, and without death there would be no new life. If people lived forever they would have no grandchildren, and again there would be no us. God can do everything but the impossible. And it is impossible to have a physical universe and life – cosmology and biology – without decay and disaster and death. This is the one palace that cannot exist without the flames.

And we have to help God put them out. This is what Judaism means when it says that God asks us to be His partners in the work of creation. No other religion and no secular philosophy has thought in these terms. "Sacred discontent" is the most radical contribution Judaism made to the civilisation of the West, and it is very challenging, very distinctive.

Which is, I suspect, why so many Jews became doctors fighting disease, or lawyers fighting injustice, or economists fighting poverty, or teachers fighting ignorance, or campaigners fighting intolerance and oppression. Jews don't accept the world. We try to mend the world, knowing how deeply it is fractured. That too is why I am proud to be a Jew.

LETTER 13:
Prayer

Rabbi, explain prayer to me. To me it seems either wish fulfilment or make-believe to think that because we say certain words, the world is going to change. Life isn't like that, and we know it isn't. So what is prayer if not belief in magic or mystery? Sorry to be so blunt, but that's what I feel.

Ruth

IF WE THINK OF PRAYER as a way of changing God's mind, then you are right, Ruth. In fact, it can't be that, for an obvious reason. Let us suppose I pray for something. Either it is good that this happens, or it is not. If it is, then God does not need my prayer to make it happen. He will make it happen anyway because it is good and God is good. If it isn't good, then God will not bring it about, however hard I pray.

The proof is none other than Moses. When Moses prayed for God to forgive the Israelites, God forgave them because God forgives. But when he prayed that he, Moses, be allowed to cross the Jordan and enter the Promised Land, God did not grant him his request. He told him to stop praying. It was not going to happen however hard or long Moses prayed. So prayer does not change God's mind in any simple sense.

Prayer changes the world because it changes us. The Hebrew word for "to pray" is *lehitpallel,* which means "to judge yourself." That is what we do when we pray. We pray not simply for God to fulfil our desires but in order to know what to desire. All animals act to satisfy their desires. Only human beings are capable of standing back and passing judgment on their desires. There are some desires we should not satisfy. Junk food is bad for us. So is smoking. So are many drugs. So is wealth illicitly obtained. So is ambition achieved by betraying others. And so on. To be humanly mature is to know what to desire.

Prayer is the education of desire. Take the weekday *Amida* as an example: It teaches us to seek knowledge, wisdom, and understanding – not just a new car, an exotic holiday, or expensive clothes. It teaches us to want to return to God when, as happens so often, we drift in the winds of time, blown this way and that by the pressures of today. It teaches us to seek spiritual healing as well as physical health. It teaches us to seek the best not just for ourselves but also for our people and ultimately for all humanity.

In *Birkot HaShaḥar,* the Dawn Blessings, prayer opens our eyes to the wonders of the physical world. It trains us to give thanks for the sheer gift of being alive. In *Pesukei DeZimra,* the Verses of Praise, we learn to see the Creator through creation. We sense the song of the earth in the wind that moves the trees, the clouds that dapple the sky, the sun that melts the snow. We hear God's praise in the breath of all that lives.

In the *Shema* we cover our eyes to move inward to the world of sound, to listen to the voice of God that we can only hear in the silence of the soul. And the word we hear is love – our love for God, His love for us. Then in the *Amida* we stand in God's presence, take three steps forward and bow. *Lehavdil* – which means, we are implying no comparison – it's like the feeling people have when they meet the Queen. You know you are in the presence of majesty. That's what a Jew feels – any Jew, any day – when he or she begins the "Standing Prayer."

Prayer teaches us to give thanks. There's a famous and fascinating piece of medical research known as the Nun Study. A group of nuns in America gave permission for their way of life to be studied in the interests of medical science. What the researchers found, comparing the nuns now with the brief autobiographies they had written sixty years before on entering the order, is that those who at the age of twenty expressed the most gratitude, lived longer and suffered fewer illnesses than their less appreciative counterparts. Giving thanks – in Hebrew, *Modim anaḥnu lakh* – generates spiritual happiness which in turn helps physical health.

Above all, prayer tells us we are not alone in the world. When Natan (then Anatoly) Sharansky was imprisoned by the KGB, his wife Avital gave him a little Hebrew book of Psalms. The KGB sensed it would give him strength, so they confiscated it. He fought a three-year campaign to have it returned, and eventually it was.

Natan's knowledge of Hebrew was limited, but he was a brilliant mathematician, so he acted as if the book was written in a code he had to decipher. Slowly he decoded it, word by word, until he arrived at a complete sentence that came to him as a revelation, as if it had been spoken specifically to him there in the Russian prison. It was a line from Psalm 23: "Though I walk through the valley of the shadow of death I will fear no evil for You are with me." Many years later he took one of these phrases as the title of his autobiography: *Fear No Evil.* To pray is to know that "You are with me." It is to know we are not alone.

Without a vessel to contain a blessing, there can be no blessing. If we have no receptacle to catch the rain, the rain may fall, but we will have none to drink. If we have no radio receiver, the sound waves will flow, but we will be unable to convert them into sound. God's blessings flow continuously, but unless we make ourselves into a vessel for them, they will flow elsewhere. Prayer is the act of turning ourselves into a vehicle for the Divine.

Prayer is to the soul what exercise is to the body. You can live without exercise but it will not be a healthy life. You can live without prayer, but whole areas of human experience will be closed to you. Prayer changes the world because it changes us, opening our eyes to the radiance of God's world, our ears to the still small voice of God's word.

LETTER 14:
On Ritual

You have told us about Judaism's great ideas. But how does that connect with the sheer detail of Judaism, the complex of laws about what we may eat and what not, what we are allowed to do on Shabbat and what is forbidden, the 613 commandments and all the rest. Isn't Judaism in danger of not seeing the forest for the trees, the grand design in the multiplicity of rules and regulations?

Yours, Ruth

LET ME RECOMMEND to you, Ruth, the spate of recent books, from Malcolm Gladwell's *Outliers* to Matthew Syed's *Bounce,* on what makes great people great. What is it that some have and the rest of us don't, whether in sport, literature, music, or science?

It's a key question and there are some fascinating stories on the way to an answer. Syed, for example, tells us that there was once a street in Reading that contained more young table tennis champions than the rest of Britain put together. He should know. He was one of them.

Then there was the Hungarian Laszlo Polgar who decided, even before getting married, that his children would become chess champions. Eventually he had three daughters and they did all become chess-playing stars.

Clearly, then, genius can't all be in the genes. There is no reason to suppose that a table tennis gene suddenly appeared at a particular time and place in Berkshire. The answer turns out to be the neuroscientific equivalent of the old joke. A tourist stops a taxi driver and asks how you get to the Royal Festival Hall. The taxi driver replies: "Practise, lady, practise."

Which is what champions do. They simply put in more hours than anyone else. The magic number is ten thousand hours. That – roughly ten years of "deep practice" – is what it takes to reach the top in almost every field.

Even Mozart, the classic example of a child prodigy, turns out to confirm the rule. Mozart's father, Leopold, was a considerable musician himself, as well as a dominating parent who forced young Wolfgang Amadeus to practise music constantly from the age of three. Although he achieved brilliance as a performer by the age of six, it was not until his early twenties that he was composing works of genius.

What is new in all this is our understanding of the neuroscience involved. Each new skill reconfigures the brain, creating new neural pathways. It seems that a substance in the brain known as myelin, whose function was previously not well understood, wraps itself around these pathways, making the connections speedier the more they are used.

The result is that practice makes certain responses immediate and intuitive, bypassing the slow, deliberative circuits in the brain. That accounts for the speed with which a Novak Djokovic or a Roger Federer can deliver a blinding return of serve. The more you practise the less need you have for conscious thought. That's why after years of driving we no longer need to think about gear changes the way we did when we were still learners.

None of these authors, as far as I know, has applied their findings to religion, but they have huge implications for the very thing you asked about, Ruth: ritual.

People tend to think that what differentiates religious people from their secular counterparts is that they believe different things. But that is less than half the story. Religious people *behave* distinctively. They engage in ritual. They do certain things like praying, over and over again. Ritual is the religious equivalent of "deep practice." *All great achievement requires ritual.*

We now understand why. Constant practice creates new neural pathways. It makes certain forms of behaviour instinctive. It reconfigures our character so that we are no longer the people we once were. We have, engraved into our instincts the way certain strokes are engraved in the minds of tennis champions, specific responses to circumstance. Ritual changes the world by changing us.

That, wrote Moses Maimonides, is the purpose of "most of the commandments." Repetition creates deeply embedded habits. Prayer engenders gratitude. Daily charitable giving makes us generous. The sexual ethic of Judaism trains us to keep check on our libido, helping us to avoid the sexual harassment that wrecks the lives of its victims and brings great careers crashing to the ground. Each of Judaism's "Thou shalt nots" teaches us self-control. Even Sigmund Freud, not a fan of religion, recognised the power of Judaism to create the habits of "instinctual renunciation" that he saw as the basis of morality and society.

Far from being outmoded, religious ritual turns out to be deeply in tune with the new neuroscience of human talent, personality, and the plasticity of the brain. Judaism never forgot what science is helping us rediscover: that ritual creates new habits of the heart that can lift us to unexpected greatness.

LETTER 15: Serving God Is Hard Work

Are you serious, Rabbi? Can keeping Shabbat, or *kashrut*, or the laws of *mikve*, really change our personality?

Ruth

YES, I AM ABSOLUTELY SERIOUS. I was once asked by the novelist Howard Jacobson why Judaism seemed so obsessed by details. Caught off guard, I didn't ask him the obvious question. "Howard, how do you write a novel that wins the Booker Prize?"

The answer, as any novelist will tell you, is hard work. You have to write every day (except Shabbat and Yom Tov) whether you feel like it or not. You have to turn writing into a ritual. And you have to worry endlessly about the details. Is this character convincing? Does the dialogue fit? Does the plot creak at this point or that? There is no great achievement in any field without ritual, routine, and attention to detail almost to the point of obsession. Genius is 1 percent inspiration, 99 percent perspiration.

The same applies to matters of the spirit. It was Judaism's greatness to understand this simple truth. Some people think faith is like talent: either you have it or you don't. But even talent is not like that: that is the point of all those recent books I mentioned in my last email. Judaism says we are all capable of spiritual greatness. Moses Maimonides even says in his law code (*Hilkhot Teshuva* 5:2): "Anyone can be as righteous as Moses." But for that, you have to work at it as hard as Moses did. Not accidentally did Judaism call serving God *avoda,* which means "hard work."

In truth, *nowhere does hard work bring more blessings than in the life of the spirit.* Here's a thought experiment, Ruth. You are just about to accept a job with one firm when a rival firm comes to you and says, "We will pay you double, on one condition: that you never read a book, listen to a piece of music, watch a play or film, or have a conversation unrelated to your work. You see, we want you to give 100 percent of your concentration to your job."

Would you accept? Obviously not. You don't have to be Jewish to know that whatever price you are offered, do not sell your soul. Better, said John Stuart Mill, to be Socrates dissatisfied than to be a fool satisfied. Spiritual pleasures are the highest of all. They are what makes us human. And no faith, no civilisation, worked harder at the life of the spirit than Judaism with its multiplicity of commands and its intricacy of detail.

And it changes lives in the most extraordinary ways. Here are three simple examples. First: Still today, Jews give to charity out of all proportion to their numbers. That is a habit born and sustained for more than three thousand years since the ancient laws of tithes, and corners of the field, and forgotten sheaves, and the remission of debts every seven years, and all the other forms of *tzedaka*, charity, so central to Jewish life.

Second: Even secular Jews cherish study, scholarship, and the life of the mind. Think of the great Jewish intellects of the modern world: in physics Einstein, in sociology Durkheim, in anthropology Levi-Strauss, in philosophy Isaiah Berlin, in literature Proust, Kafka, Bashevis Singer, Agnon, Bellow, and Roth; Jews made up 22 percent of all Nobel Prize-winners in the twentieth century, 49 percent of world chess masters, and this from a population numbering 0.2 percent of the population of the world – a disproportion of more than a hundred times. As Sergey Brin, cofounder of Google, once put it: "We came from one of those Russian Jewish families where you expected even the plumber to have a PhD." Where did this come from if not from a religion that made study, *talmud Torah*, a religious duty even higher than prayer?

Third: Jews were distinguished throughout history for having exceptionally strong families. From where did this come if not from the structure of Jewish law that sanctifies the home, cherishes the love between husband and wife, parent and child, and invests everything to do with marriage with the charisma of holiness?

Judaism transforms Jews – so much so that even Jews several generations removed from religious practice still carry with them the habits of the heart and disciplines of the mind that were born and sustained in the life of the commandments. They are living off inherited capital. But it's always better to make your own spiritual wealth and teach your children how to do so. Which means Judaism and its daily disciplines.

LETTER 16:
Antisemitism Returns

Rabbi, let me change the subject if I may. Why has antisemitism returned? Surely if there was one thing on which everyone agreed after the Holocaust, it was "Never again." But now it seems more like "Ever again." This really troubles me.

Yours, Michael

THIS IS ONE of the most serious questions of our time. Let's first step back and consider what antisemitism is. It is not a coherent doctrine. In the nineteenth century Jews were hated because they were rich and because they were poor, because they were capitalists and because they were communists, because they kept to themselves and because they infiltrated everywhere. Voltaire hated them because they believed in an ancient, to him superstitious, faith. Stalin hated them because they were "rootless cosmopolitans" who believed nothing.

Antisemitism is not a belief. It is a sickness and one that has little to do with Jews. Let me explain. The world is constantly changing, and change is very hard for people to bear, especially when they experience it as a form of loss. The easiest way of coping with it is to blame someone else. In the wilderness the Israelites did this to Moses. The fact that he had liberated them from slavery was irrelevant. They accused him of bringing them out into the desert to die.

Blame is a sickness and a very dangerous one. It defines you as a victim. It absolves you of responsibility. It allows you to say that the problems you are experiencing are someone else's fault, and were it not for them you would not now be suffering. This is false and ultimately self-destructive, but it is a comforting thing to believe.

Who then do you blame? Someone who is (a) close enough to be a plausible candidate, (b) different enough to be not like you, and (c) harmless or weak or forgiving enough for it not to be dangerous to blame them. No one blames those they genuinely fear.

For centuries Jews filled that role in Christian Europe. They were religiously different. In the nineteenth century they were deemed to be racially different. Today they fulfil that role in an Islamic Middle East. They are not Arab. They are not Muslim. They are different.

Antisemitism is a projection, and is caused not by Jews but by internal conflicts in the societies that give rise to it. Today the Middle East, and to some degree Europe, are riven by conflict. The world is changing, economically, politically, and technologically almost faster than people can bear. So they search for someone to blame. It can be the West; it can be America; or it can be the Jews. Since Jews are smaller and weaker than the West or America, it usually lands up being them.

A thousand years of Christian and European antisemitism gave rise to a long series of myths, from the blood libel to *The Protocols of the Elders of Zion*. After the Holocaust people began to realise how murderous these falsehoods were, and by and large Europe was cured of them.

The trouble is that by then Europe had infected the Middle East with just these myths. The blood libel was taken to Egypt and Syria by Coptic and Maronite Christians in the early nineteenth century. *The Protocols of the Elders of Zion* was taken by the mufti of Jerusalem direct from Nazi Germany. These myths are alive and well today and have been broadcast by Egyptian and Syrian television as well as other official and influential media.

Antisemitism is a deadly doctrine. It endangers Jews. But it also ultimately destroys antisemitic societies themselves. The reason should be obvious. When you blame others and define yourself as a victim, you abdicate responsibility for solving your own problems. That is why medieval Christendom, Nazi Germany, Czarist Russia, and the Soviet Union – massive powers in their day – died from internal decay. You cannot build a viable religion, society, or identity on prejudice. Hate endangers the hated but it destroys the hater.

In the last month of his life, Moses gave the Israelites an unusual command. He said, "Do not hate an Egyptian, for you were strangers in his land" (Deut. 23:8). What did he mean? The Egyptians enslaved the Israelites and tried to kill every male child. Was that a reason not to hate them? Surely the opposite was the case.

What Moses was doing was very profound. He was telling the next generation that if they continued to hate Egyptians, they would still be slaves – to the past, to resentment, to a sense of grievance. Moses would have taken the Israelites out of Egypt but he would not have taken Egypt out of the Israelites. He was stating one of the deepest truths of all: *If you want to be free, you have to let go of hate.*

That is a message we must insist on at every opportunity. Antisemitism matters not because Jews are Jews but because Jews are human. You cannot deny someone else's humanity without endangering your own.

LETTER 17:
The Assault on Israel

Rabbi, do you see criticism of Israel, of the kind we are experiencing on campus today, as antisemitism?

Ruth

WE MUST BE VERY CAREFUL, Ruth, not to use words lightly. To regard all criticism of Israel as antisemitism is simply wrong. It depends on the criticism.

Criticism of Israel is of five kinds. First there is the criticism every nation receives because none is perfect. Living with such criticism is part of democratic freedom, and Israel is a democracy.

Second is the criticism that comes from siding with the underdog, with David against Goliath. Once Israel was seen as the David, the small nation surrounded by large enemies. After its victory in the Six-Day War, that tide slowly changed. Today Israel is seen as the Goliath, the Palestinians as David. We have to live with that. Better an Israel that is strong, safe, and criticised than one that is weak, vulnerable, and elicits people's sympathy.

Third, there is criticism that is simply ignorant of the facts, the most significant being the claim that Israel is an obstacle to peace. In fact, in the 1920s and 1930s there were various plans for the partition of the land into two states, one Jewish, one Arab. Jews accepted them; the Arabs rejected them. In 1947, the United Nations voted for partition. Again, Jews accepted, the Arabs refused. David Ben-Gurion reiterated the call for peace as a central part of Israel's Declaration of Independence in May 1948. Israel's neighbours – Egypt, Jordan, Syria, Lebanon, and Iraq – responded by attacking it on all fronts.

The offer was renewed in 1967 after the Six-Day War. The response of the Arab League, meeting in Khartoum in September 1967, was the famous "Three Nos": no to peace, no to negotiations, no to the recognition of the State of Israel. The call was repeated many times by Golda Meir, and always decisively rejected.

The boldest offer was made by Ehud Barak at Taba in 2001. It offered the Palestinians a state in the whole of Gaza and 97 percent of the West Bank, with border compensations for the other 3 percent, with East Jerusalem as its capital. Many members of the Palestinian team wanted to accept. Yasser Arafat refused.

The obstacle to peace from the 1920s to today has been the refusal of the Palestinians and their supporters to grant Israel legitimacy, the right to exist. You cannot – logically cannot – make peace with one who denies your right to exist. Peace is more than a resting-place on the road to war.

Fourth, there is criticism that is not simply ignorant but wilfully ignorant, deliberately misleading. One such is the claim that Israel is racist, an apartheid state. In fact in Israeli hospitals people of all faiths and ethnicities are treated alike. All have the vote. All can attend Israeli universities. All can be elected to and take their place in the Knesset.

A Druze Arab, Majalli Wahabi, briefly served as president of Israel after Moshe Katsav's resignation while acting head of state Dalia Itzik was out of the country. A Christian Arab, George Karra, headed the panel of judges that tried and found guilty Israel's President Katsav. None of these is conceivable in an apartheid state.

Meanwhile in December 2010 Palestinian Authority President Mahmoud Abbas declared: "We have frankly said, and always will say: If there is an independent Palestinian state with Jerusalem as its capital, we won't agree to the presence of one Israeli in it." This vision of a *Judenrein* Palestine really is racist.

Fifth is principled anti-Zionism of the kind embraced by Hamas, Hezbollah, and Iran which sees the destruction of Israel as a matter of non-negotiable religious principle. This is pure supersessionist theology of the kind practised by the church for many centuries, and is classic anti-Judaism. In a world in which there are eighty-two Christian states and fifty-six Islamic ones, it says that Jews alone are not entitled to a home of their own.

Interwoven with the fourth and fifth types of criticism are all the classic antisemitic myths, from the blood libel to *The Protocols of the Elders of Zion*.

All this should concern us for many reasons. First, some of it is antisemitic, increasingly so. Second, hate-filled rhetoric is being allowed on British and American campuses in the name of academic freedom. This is not academic freedom, which means the freedom to hold and express your views without fear, even when they run against the consensus. This freedom from intimidation is being denied to defenders of Israel today.

Academic freedom means the willingness to let all sides of the argument be respectfully heard. Manifestly this is not happening. What is happening was best described by Julian Benda in his famous book *Le Trahison des Clercs,* "The Treason of the Intellectuals." In it he said that the academy had ceased to be a place for the pursuit of truth and had become an arena for "the intellectual organisation of political hatreds." He wrote those words in 1927. Reflect on what happened a few years later.

Refusal to give Israel a fair hearing will not bring peace, will not help the Palestinians, and will do great damage to the cause of freedom in the Middle East. The Arab Spring of 2011 showed how dictatorial are the regimes of the countries that have been in the forefront of hostility to Israel. That is because historically antisemitism, and now anti-Zionism, have been the weapons of choice of dictators seeking to deflect criticism of their own rule.

We can state the consequence in a simple sentence: *Those who deny Israel's freedom will never achieve their own.*

None of this should stop us supporting all initiatives for peace and working for a Middle East in which all people, of every ethnicity and faith, have freedom, dignity, and security.

LETTER 18:
God of Life, Book of Life

Rabbi, we have more questions but we've decided to save them for now and simply ask you: What is your message to us in the year to come?

Ruth and Michael

RUTH, MICHAEL, one of the great lines of our prayers – it comes from Psalm 90 – says, "Teach us to number our days that we may get a heart of wisdom." As Steve Jobs once said, "Your time is limited, so don't waste it living someone else's life." Don't try to be what you aren't. Try to be what you are called on to be.

I have seen people achieve great success and yet end their lives sad and lonely because they thought about themselves and never really cared for others. I have seen people with great talent underachieve because they never fully realised that character matters more than talent, and wisdom more than being clever. I have seen people accumulate great wealth without finding happiness because they forgot that wealth is only a means, not an end. Happiness is made by the good we do, the relationships we form, and the extent to which we enhance the lives of others.

There is massive research evidence that people who are religious are happier, healthier, and live longer than others; not always – there are many exceptions – but on average. It's obvious why. Religion encourages us to sustain marriages, strengthen families, become part of a community, and do good to others by giving, *tzedaka,* or volunteering, *ḥesed.* Faith endows our life with meaning.

I do not mean to criticise anyone who chooses otherwise, nor to suggest that religious people are any less prone than others to the "thousand natural shocks that flesh is heir to." But I have found that faith has helped me and many others I know to survive crisis, avoid temptation, live for the things that matter, and work daily to mend the faults I know I have and the mistakes I know I make. Faith speaks to the better angels of our nature.

It makes a difference to keep Shabbat and know that, yes, work is important, but there are limits. Society forgets those limits. It treats employees and professionals as if they were permanently on call, ready to respond 24/7 to emails and phone calls. It forgets that there are limits to our consumption and our pursuit of desire. The Sages asked, "Why is God called *Shaddai* (one of the names of God in the Torah)?" They answered, "Because He said to the world, *Dai,* enough." There are times when we have to say to the world, "Enough," when we don't work or spend or answer the phone but instead enjoy our family, celebrate community, and thank God for His blessings.

It makes a difference to *daven*, to pray, to be in regular touch with the Presence at the heart of being, to give voice to our hopes, thanks for our lives, and expression to our emotions, joining our voice to the choral symphony of our people as it sings its song of praise to God.

It makes a difference to have days like Yom Kippur when we can acknowledge our shortcomings, make amends for our failures, apologise, and know we are forgiven.

It makes a difference to share a faith and a tradition with your children and know that what you live for will live on – that you are in fact part of the longest and most remarkable story ever written by one nation since man first set foot on earth.

In the end a life must have meaning, and we can never find meaning in isolation. Think of a letter in the alphabet. All meaning is expressed in words and all words are made of letters. But no letter has meaning on its own. To have meaning it must be joined to others to make words, sentences, paragraphs, and stories. The same is true of lives. No life has meaning on its own. It must be joined to other lives in families, communities, peoples, and their histories. Our individualistic age often forgets this but Judaism never does.

And yes, bad things are happening in the world today, but the good things outweigh them. Yes, Israel is criticised, even isolated, but at least we have an Israel – a land, a home, a state, a society – after two thousand years of exile.

Yes, there is antisemitism. But there is much philosemitism also. Jews and Judaism are respected as perhaps never before. Recent research in the United States, for example, showed that Americans feel more warmly towards Jews than they do towards the members of any other religious group.

And yes, Jewish life is not always as consistently inspiring as we would wish it to be. The way to change that is to get involved and make it better.

As I write these words, Ruth and Michael, I celebrate twenty years as chief rabbi. It's strange to think that I began this task around the time you were born. In those years I have met Jews of all kinds throughout the world. And if I have noticed one thing it is that Jews seem somehow more vivid, more energetic and passionate, hungrier for life, than most others.

The reason is not that Jews are different. It's that Judaism is different.

Jews found God in life – not in a distant heaven or the World to Come or a monastic retreat or a world-denying asceticism. God, said Moses, is not distant but close. Forgive the expression, but Jews always treated God – and by the evidence of the Torah He has treated us – as if we were close relatives, part of the *mishpaḥa*. Perhaps that's why we so often argued with Him, and He with us. But relatives are inseparable. You can argue with a member of the family but he remains a member of the family. In Judaism, God is near. The bond between us is unbreakable.

God is close. God is here. God is life. Therefore celebrate life. Sanctify life. Turn life into a blessing and make a blessing over life. That is Judaism in twenty-five words.

I promise you that whatever you choose to do, living a Jewish life will help you do it better, with greater balance, more wisdom, more joy, a deeper sense of purpose, and a feeling of having been touched by eternity.

Ruth, Michael, may the God of life write you in the Book of Life, and may your life become a blessed chapter in His book.

CONVERSATION

This section contains a five-part series of mini booklets entitled *Little Books of Big Questions*, originally published in September 2007 in partnership with the Union of Jewish Students. The series was written following a discussion with student leaders who were troubled by questions that typically concern young people. These readings are a way of sharing the conversation, the questions and answers, and the ideas discussed on that day.

INTRODUCTION TO LITTLE BOOKS OF BIG QUESTIONS

We were sitting together round the table in our home, after the reception Elaine and I give each year for the leadership of Union of Jewish Students and National Union of Students. The years 2006–2007 had been tough years – the academic boycott, deepening criticism of Israel, and a general unease about terror and religious radicalism. It was a bad year for religion in general, with books on atheism becoming best-sellers.

The Jewish student leaders seemed troubled, so we asked them to stay behind and simply talk about what was on their mind. These pamphlets are summarised accounts of what we spoke about.

The names of the students have been changed.

Being Jewish in the Twenty-First Century

Philip began by raising the most fundamental question of all. Why be Jewish at all in the twenty-first century? Haven't we given the world everything Judaism first taught: freedom, human dignity, rights? Do we really need religion in an age of science? Do we really need to stay different, special, set apart? Don't we need, on the contrary, to learn how to live together? Isn't Judaism simply outmoded in a secular age?

I don't think so. There is something in the human condition that aspires beyond the secular, the material, the visible and quantifiable. We may be "dust of the earth" but we have immortal longings. We are the meaning-seeking animal. Only *Homo sapiens* can imagine a world other than the one we currently live in. We are the only beings able to construct sentences in the future tense. We are the one life form known to us in the universe capable of asking the question "Why?"

The "why" questions ask us to lift up our eyes beyond the immediate, in search of the ultimate. The name we give to the ultimate is God. The search for meaning is the religious quest, and more than any other faith, Judaism has given expression to it. In the fine words of the Catholic writer Paul Johnson, "No people has ever insisted more firmly than the Jews that history has a purpose and humanity a destiny.... The Jews, therefore, stand right at the centre of the perennial attempt to give human life the dignity of a purpose." Life is more than the money we earn, the car we drive, the clothes we wear. Religion is the space we make in our life for the things that are important, not just urgent.

The unbroken role of Judaism for forty centuries has been to lift our sights beyond the status quo and say: There is better way. We are the iconoclasts, the people with the courage to challenge the idols of the age, whatever the idols, whatever the age. Judaism is the countervoice in the human conversation. When people worshipped power, Judaism stood up for the powerless. When 90 percent of Europe was illiterate, Jews cared about education. When the vast majority of humanity lived in poverty, Judaism practised the principle of *tzedaka*, the duty on those who have more than they need to share with those who have less. So it is today. The idols change. But the Jewish duty to show there is another way has not changed.

So what is "the other way" today?

The other way is to say that all we have created in the twenty-first century is a means, not an end. Our economic advances mean that we can address the poverty of a world in which a billion people live without adequate food, shelter, and medical resources. Our medical advances mean that we can begin to do something about the thirty thousand children who die every day from preventable diseases. Our technological advances mean that we can use the Internet to bring knowledge to the 115 million children who today go without any education at all.

But that has nothing to do with religion, let alone Judaism. Really? The debt relief programme that led directly to Make Poverty History was called Jubilee 2000, and was based directly on the debt relief provisions of the Torah set out in (Leviticus) chapter 25. We live in a culture all of whose values were originally religious. We've simply forgotten that fact.

It was Judaism, the Hebrew Bible, that first broke with myth and taught that the world was the product of a single creative will, thus preparing the way for science. It was Judaism that first taught that every human being, Black, white, rich, poor, weak, strong, is in God's image, thus laying the basis for a free society. It was Judaism that first taught that God, after the Flood, made a covenant with all humanity, thus creating the idea of global human solidarity.

These ideas emerged in the Judaeo-Christian West, nowhere else. They are unique to the civilisation built on the values of the Tanakh (Bible) – the values that made their way into European culture with the birth of printing, the spread of books, and the availability of Bibles translated into languages people could understand. The "modern" was biblical through and through. It's just that we've forgotten this fact.

But in that case, we're all heirs to that heritage, whether we know it or not. You certainly don't need to be religious, or Jewish, to live in today's world, whatever debts it owes to Jews or Judaism or the Bible or the past.

Not so. There is a difference between scientific truths and human truths – truths about life. The truths of science are true, and always have been, whether they have been discovered or not. The truths about human life, individual and social, exist only if we live them. If we don't, they disappear. Societies have found freedom then lost it again. Whole civilisations have disappeared. That happened to Mesopotamia, the Egypt of the Pharaohs, the Assyrians, Babylonians, Persians, the ancient Greeks and Romans, and so on all the way to Soviet communism. They exist today only in history books and museums. Virtually the only cultures that have ever lasted, undiminished, are Judaism and the two other religions based on it: Christianity and Islam.

If we lose Judaism, we will eventually lose Western civilisation and everything associated with it. If you doubt the capacity of civilisations to destroy themselves, just read Jared Diamond's books *The Third Chimpanzee* and *Collapse.*

Are you serious? The future of Western civilisation depends on my being Jewish?

Yes, it sounds crazy, over-dramatic and self-serving.

Yet Europe is dying. There is not a single European nation that has anywhere near replacement birth rates. That is because of the collapse of marriage in the course of a single generation. Freedom of expression is dying in British universities, the result of the twin impact of political correctness and academic boycotts. The delicate ecological balance of the earth is dying because we've forgotten the lessons of Shabbat and the Sabbatical year: the principle that there must be limits to our exploitation of the earth and its resources. Judaism has seen every major civilisation outside the Far East – forces that seemed invulnerable in their day – collapse and die.

It alone survives. Why the Jews?

I believe the answer has to do with divine providence; but at a human level it may simply be because, as the Torah says, we are the obstinate, stiff-necked people who refused to do what everyone else was doing, because we had the courage to believe in the dignity of difference. We didn't go with the flow. We kept faith – with God, with our ancestors, with our covenant of destiny. Somehow, in some obscure way, a series of truths about the human situation – the truths we call Torah – got hold of us and never let us go. And humanity needs those truths. Not just in a book, but in lives – in your life and mine.

You're asking me to believe that whether or not I live as a Jew is going to make a difference not just to me but to humanity?

I don't ask you to do anything I haven't done myself. I did not go to university expecting to discover my Jewish identity. In fact, it was there that it was really challenged. Yet it was there that I discovered the truths that changed my life: that if I didn't stay Jewish, my entire family history – more than a hundred generations – would come to an end with me. My ancestors prayed for freedom. Should I, having found it, take what they lived for and throw it away? Jews were prepared to die for their faith. Was I unprepared even to live for it?

So I made my choice: to live as a Jew and learn about Judaism. Almost without thinking about it, I discovered the path to personal meaning: through our marriage, the family we created, the communities we helped build, the connections we made with Jews throughout the world, and the way we lit our lives by the mitzvot (commandments) we kept. And I wrote about the problems of today, and discovered that our heritage really does speak not only to Jews but to non-Jews also.

Judaism is our family heritage – our equivalent of a Leonardo painting, acquired by a distant ancestor, handed on from one generation to the next – and now it's ours. Could I really give it away? Throw it away? Sell it – knowing that in truth, it's priceless? That's what Judaism is and more. And right now, its future is in your hands.

For further reading

My own book on this subject is *Radical Then, Radical Now* (2004).

Alternatively, try:
James Kugel, *On Being a Jew* (1998),
Emil Fackenheim, *What Is Judaism?* (1999),
Herman Wouk, *This Is My God* (1992), and
Daniel Gordis, *Does the World Need the Jews?* (1997).

Why the Jews? Confronting Modern Antisemitism

Rachel was worried about the return of antisemitism and anti-Zionism to campus life: the Close space motions, the calls for an academic boycott, the religious and political radicalism that seemed now, as in the past, to blame Jews or Israel for the troubles of the world. Nothing had really prepared her for this, and she wanted to understand why it was happening.

What is antisemitism and why does it keep coming back?
Antisemitism is the paradigm case of dislike of the unlike. Long ago, when people lived in bands or small city-states, they feared the stranger. In fact, in many languages, the word for "stranger" and "enemy" are the same. That fear once had survival value. There are many cases in which trusting local populations received European strangers as friends, only to find themselves attacked, robbed, and enslaved. It happened to the Incas and Aztecs, for example, at the hands of

the Spanish in the early sixteenth century. So people learned to fear the stranger.

Jews were born as a people in the opposite experience. They were feared by the Egyptians, perhaps (so some historians have argued) because Egypt had once been conquered by an earlier group of strangers known as the Hyksos. To neutralise a possible threat, the Egyptians enslaved the Israelites. So the Israelites knew what it was like to be on the receiving end of hatred.

On achieving their freedom, Moses turned this experience around to create one of the greatest of all moral principles: "Do not oppress the stranger because you know what it feels like to be a stranger: you were once strangers in Egypt" (Ex. 23:9). Thirty-six times in the Torah we are commanded to love the stranger. That is the single most important rule in the entire lexicon of morality.

But everyone is a stranger to someone else. Why the Jews? Until relatively recently, most societies imposed a single religion, a single culture. Those who did not belong to that religion or culture lacked rights. Most people simply adopted the religion of the majority. Jews – at least, most Jews, most of the time – did not. So they were an anomaly. They were different and stayed different. They believed in the right and duty to be true to your faith even though most people in society don't share it.

That made them exceptionally vulnerable to the dislike of the unlike; fear of, and hostility to, strangers. In Christian Europe Jews were the archetypal strangers. Their vulnerability was compounded by the fact that they lacked rights. They couldn't vote; they couldn't take part in government; they had no power – and they had no home in the sense defined by the poet Robert Frost as "the place where, when you have to go there, they have to take you in." By and large, people only attack those they can attack with impunity. Because Jews lacked the full protection of the law, they could be assaulted, often without fear of reprisal.

But that was then. Why now? And why Israel?

Because Israel in the world today is like the Jew in Europe until the Holocaust: a stranger. It is a very small, very vulnerable country in a part of the world whose culture, religion, and political institutions are different.

But that is only part of the answer. Antisemitism, though ancient, was not continuous. It appeared at times of great stress, when societies were going through massive and disorienting change. A good example is the witch hunts of the fourteenth to the sixteenth century. Throughout Europe, tens of thousands of women were tried and burned as witches. We have no idea why other than that, first, the Middle Ages were coming to an end, and second, women, usually living alone, were exceptionally vulnerable.

The world today is undergoing some of the most rapid and far-reaching changes in all of history: the complex set of phenomena known as globalisation. Change creates insecurity, which generates fear, which gives rise to hate. Hate will always find as its object something or someone who is different and vulnerable. For every Jew today there are 183 Christians and one hundred Muslims. That makes Jews, now as in the past, vulnerable.

So what should be our response?

Our first response should be to heed the famous words of Rabbi Nahman of Breslov: "The whole world is a very narrow bridge, and the main thing is never to be afraid." We must be vigilant. We must fight antisemitism wherever we find it. But we must not be afraid. Fear is dysfunctional. It paralyses and demoralises. Among the most beautiful lines in the Bible are the opening words of Psalm 27: "The Lord is my light and my salvation – whom then shall I fear? The Lord is the stronghold of my life – of whom shall I be afraid?" That is part of what faith is: the refusal to give way to fear.

The second response is to fight falsehood with truth, and hate with love. Antisemitism happens to Jews, but it is not who we are. Historically we never defined ourselves as a people hated by gentiles; we saw ourselves as a people loved by God. No people should ever allow itself to be defined by its enemies.

One story has stayed with me ever since I first heard it. It took place in Russia in the early 1990s, following the collapse of communism. For the first time in seventy years, Jews were free openly to live as Jews, but at the same time antisemitic attitudes, long suppressed, also came to the surface.

A British rabbi had gone there to help with the reconstruction of Jewish life. One day he was visited by a young woman in distress. "All my life," she said, "I hid the fact that I was a Jew and no one ever commented on my Jewishness. Now, though, when I walk past, my neighbours mutter *Zhid* [Jew]. What shall I do?"

The rabbi thought for a minute, then replied, "If you had not told me you were Jewish, I would never have known.

But with my hat and beard, no one could miss the fact that I am a Jew. Yet, in all the months I have been here, no one has shouted *Zhid* at me. Why do you think that is?"

The woman was silent and then said, "Because they know that if they shout *Zhid* at me, I will take it as an insult, but if they shout *Zhid* at you, you will take it as a compliment." That is a deep insight. Beyond eternal vigilance, the best way for Jews to combat antisemitism is to wear their identity with pride.

But how does that help? Being proud to be Jewish won't stop antisemitism.

We, on our own, cannot cure antisemitism. The victim cannot cure the crime. The hated cannot cure the hate. The cure for antisemitism exists only within the cultures that give rise to it and tolerate it. Fortunately, as the result of a generation of Holocaust education, most people know where antisemitism leads. We need allies; we must actively seek them; we must not be left to fight this battle on our own.

Some years ago, when antisemitic activity on campus was beginning to rise, I called a meeting of Jewish student leaders. I said: The next few months are going to be difficult. You will find yourselves under attack. I promise that you will not be left to fight this battle alone. What I want you to do is the opposite of what people expect. I want you to lead the fight against Islamophobia and all other forms of prejudice.

Let us do what Moses told the Israelites to do: turn their experience of being a stranger into loving, not hating, the stranger.

The leader of the Jewish students at that time was a wonderful young man, Alan Senitt, tragically murdered in

Washington DC at the age of twenty-seven. By then he had become director of the Coexistence Trust, an organisation dedicated to fighting antisemitism and Islamophobia. He understood that the way to fight hate is to fight it together with other faiths, other ethnicities, with people of goodwill everywhere. No group should have to fight prejudice alone.

In the end, antisemitism – the hatred of difference – is an assault not on Jews only but on humanity as such. Life is sacred because each person – even genetically identical twins – is different, therefore irreplaceable. Because we are all different, we each have something unique to contribute to humankind.

Cultural diversity is as essential to our social ecology as is biodiversity to our natural ecology. A world without room for Jews, or for the State of Israel, is one that has no room for difference, and a world that lacks space for difference lacks space for humanity itself.

Let the final word go to Judea Pearl, father of the murdered journalist Daniel Pearl. I once asked him why he had chosen to respond to Daniel's murder by reaching out to others the hand of friendship. He replied: "Hate killed my son. Therefore, for the rest of my life, I will fight hate." That is the imperative of our time.

For further reading:

Among the best surveys of antisemitism are:

Robert S. Wistrich, *Antisemitism: The Longest Hatred* (1994) and Walter Laqueur, *The Changing Face of Anti-Semitism: From Ancient Times to the Present Day* (2008).

Also worth reading are:
Bernard Lewis, *Semites and Anti-Semites* (1999);
Rosemary Radford Ruether, *Faith and Fratricide* (1996) on Christian antisemitism; and
Norman Cohn, *Warrant for Genocide* (2006) on *The Protocols of the Elders of Zion.*

Judaism in a Multifaith Society

Jane wanted to know what I thought about interfaith dialogue. Is it something Jews should be involved in, or wary of? Is there a risk that learning about other people's beliefs may weaken our own? Just how important is it? And are there limits to dialogue?

Why has interfaith work become so important?

For much of history, most people lived among people who were like themselves: they shared the same culture, the same traditions, the same history, the same values. Today we live with difference. On an average high street or typical campus we find ourselves surrounded by more different cultures than a nineteenth-century anthropologist would have known in a lifetime. So it becomes important to understand one another and to develop a respect for diversity. The very future of free societies depends on it. And we should be taking the lead.

Why us? Do we have something special to contribute?

We do. Jews have had more experience than any other group in history of being a minority and yet sustaining our identity.

Jews have lived in most countries and cultures: in Christian Europe, Islamic North Africa and the Ottoman Empire, and among Hindus, Sikhs, and Jain in India. There were Jewish communities in many parts of Africa as well as in China. They developed a principled approach to good community relations: they called it *darkhei shalom*, "the ways of peace." But they cared too about maintaining their identity, about Jewish continuity. This is a delicate balance, one in which we have had long practice.

From each of these encounters Jews learned much, despite holding firmly to our own beliefs. As the Sages said: "If they tell you there is wisdom among the nations, believe it; if they tell you there is Torah among the nations, do not believe it." Faith is particular, wisdom universal. The talmudic Sages respected the Greeks for their astronomy, the Persians for their etiquette, the Romans for their technical expertise, while at the same time believing that the Torah is unique in its spirituality.

Two Jewish ideas are particularly important in a diverse society like ours. The first is that we have never sought to convert anyone. Friendship between faiths depends on this. The desire to convert others has led, historically, to prejudice and persecution. The second is the principle of integration without assimilation. This dates back twenty-six centuries to the prophet Jeremiah, who wrote to the Jewish exiles in Babylon: "Seek the peace and prosperity of the city to which I have carried you into exile. Pray to the Lord for it, because if it prospers, you too will prosper."

But why haven't Jews sought to convert others? Surely if Judaism is true, we should try to persuade everyone to become Jewish?

The Torah has a unique structure. It begins, for its first eleven chapters, with a history of humanity as such. Then, in Genesis chapter 12, it moves from the universal to the particular, from Noah to Abraham. So there are two covenants in Genesis, one with all humanity in the days of Noah, the other with a particular family, Abraham and Sarah and their children.

That, I believe, is true to the human situation. There are universals. Every human being needs food, clothing, shelter, access to medical treatment, and an education. Virtually every society values justice, fairness, and the rule of law. These form the basis of universal codes of human rights. They are the contemporary equivalent of the covenant with Noah.

But there are also particularities, in respect of which cultures are profoundly different. As Jews we celebrate freedom through Pesaḥ and the story of the Exodus. We honour creation and the integrity of nature by keeping Shabbat. We are a faith based on asking questions and engaging in "argument for the sake of Heaven." These things are not universal. They are what make Judaism distinctive. And we are enlarged by difference. By being true to our uniqueness, we contribute what only we can give.

So we have to balance the universal and the particular, our commonalities and differences. *If we were totally unalike, we could not communicate. If we were totally alike, we would have nothing to say*. Judaism achieves this balance by speaking of two covenants: the universal covenant with Noah and the particular covenant with Abraham. Or to put it simply: Our task is to be true to our own faith while being a blessing to others regardless of their faith.

But doesn't mixing with others risk weakening our own faith?

With few exceptions, most of us are going to come into contact with people of different faiths anyway. Complete segregation is difficult, perhaps impossible, so we each have to learn how to relate to others without losing our own heritage and identity.

Perhaps an analogy would help here. There are not many Norwegians in Washington DC, so that if you are Norwegian, it is quite likely that either you or your children will lose their identity in time. But there is one house in Washington DC that flies the Norwegian flag. On its walls are paintings of Norway. The people in the house speak Norwegian and observe all of Norway's customs and holidays. They will never assimilate.

What house is it? Right – you guessed. It is the Norwegian Embassy, and ambassadors never assimilate. Regard yourself as a Jewish ambassador and you too will not assimilate.

But do we really believe in diversity, or is it that we simply believe in exclusivity, that being Jewish means belonging to a club with only a few members?

No; we really do believe that "the righteous of the nations of the world have a share in the World to Come." The Torah gives high praise to Abraham's contemporary Melkizedek, calling him a "priest of the most high God," even though he was not part of the Abrahamic covenant. It values Moses' father-in-law Jethro, even though he was a Midianite priest. The single most blameless individual in the Tanakh (Bible), Job, is not described as Jewish. He is a kind of "everyman," the righteous counterpart of Adam.

There are two ways of learning how to be moral. One is by general rules: don't steal, don't murder, don't tell lies. The other is by particular examples: find good people, those you can admire, and see how they live. You need both. Judaism respects both. The Noah covenant is about general rules. Jews and Judaism are meant to be a particular example. That is why we believe there can be other ways of reaching heaven, and why we can respect other examples of good and Godly people.

To what extent should we engage in theological dialogue? Should everything be open to discussion?

There are universal problems that affect all of us: global warming, the overexploitation of natural resources, the growing disparities between rich and poor, the risks and benefits of new medical technologies, and so on. It is important that we come together on these issues, regardless of our particular theologies or sacred texts. Matters that affect us all should involve us all.

It is important too, for citizenship in a liberal democracy, that we make friendships across boundaries and come to understand other people's sensitivities. Jews, for example, must understand what is hurtful to Muslims; Muslims must understand what is hurtful to Jews. We win respect by showing respect: there is no other way.

But there are core beliefs that are ultimately intelligible only to those within a tradition. Those outside may "understand" them in some sense, but always as an outsider. This is like the difference between science and poetry. Science is translatable across cultures, poetry is not. There are aspects of faith that are more like poetry than science. There are elements of any faith that will always be partially incomprehensible to those outside that faith.

It was the view of the late Rabbi Joseph Soloveitchik that such core beliefs should not be made the subject of interfaith dialogue. In general, love means giving the other space to be themselves. Even in the deepest relationship, there will always be something in the other person we do not fully understand. If that is true between two individuals of the same faith, how much more so between those of different faiths? There is a margin of mystery we must respect.

How then should we be involved?

Jewish students should be in the forefront in fighting prejudice, respecting difference, and working across faiths to create a climate of mutual respect. Maintaining the balance between our commonalities and our differences is what gives liberal democracies their vitality and creativity.

After the Tower of Babel, the human condition has meant a world in which, though there is only one God, there are many languages and cultures, each with something unique to contribute to our collective heritage. We tell different stories, practise different ways of life, yet we are all created in God's image. There are many faiths but only one world in which we must learn to live together. That is our challenge, never more so than now.

For further reading

My own book, *The Dignity of Difference* (2003), is about this subject.

For other Jewish views, see:
Abraham Joshua Heschel, *No Religion Is an Island* (1966),
Irving Greenberg, *For the Sake of Heaven and Earth* (2004),
Michael Wyschogrod, *Abraham's Promise* (2004), and
David Novak, *Jewish-Christian Dialogue* (1989).

Rabbi Soloveitchik's essay "Confrontation" can be found in:
Norman Lamm and Walter Wurzburger, eds., *A Treasury of Tradition* (1967).

An important historical study is:
Jacob Katz, *Exclusiveness and Tolerance* (2021).

Israel: In Search of Peace

Paul, like many other students I've met in recent years, has been traumatised by the attacks on Israel on campus. Could it really be that the country he knows so well and loves so deeply is the same Israel that is accused of so many sins? He found himself torn and confused.

Why is Israel so important to us?

Judaism – twice as old as Christianity, three times as old as Islam – was the call to Abraham's descendants to create a society of freedom, justice, and compassion under the sovereignty of God. A society involves a land, a home, somewhere where the "children of Israel" form the majority, and can thus create a culture, an economy, a political system in accordance with their values. That land was, and is, Israel.

The Jewish connection to Israel is older by far than that of any other civilisation to a place. It goes back four thousand years to the first recorded syllables of Jewish time, God's command to Abraham: "Leave your land, your birthplace, and your father's house and go to the land that I will show you"

(Ex. 12:1). Seven times God promised Abraham the land, and repeated that promise to Isaac and Jacob. If any nation on earth has a right to any land – a right based on history, attachment, long association – then the Jewish people has a right to Israel.

But surely that right lapsed long ago, when Jews were exiled?
Jews never left Israel voluntarily. They never relinquished their rights. They returned whenever they could: in the days of Moses, then again after the Babylonian exile, then again in generation after generation. Judah HaLevi went there in the twelfth century. So did Maimonides and his family, though they found it impossible to stay. Nahmanides went there in 1265. There was a large community there in the sixteenth century. There are places, especially in the Galilee, where they never left at all. My great-grandfather, Rabbi Arye Leib Frumkin, went to Israel in 1871; his father had settled there twenty years earlier.

But that is our story. Surely not everyone saw it the same way.
Those with a sense of history long ago recognised the injustice of denying Jews their ancestral home. In 1799, Napoleon at the start of his Middle East campaign called on Jews to return (the campaign failed before there was a chance to act on this proposal). So did many British thinkers in the nineteenth century, among them Lord Palmerston, Lord Shaftesbury, and the novelist George Eliot (in her novel *Daniel Deronda*).

The Balfour Declaration in 1917, ratified in 1920 by the League of Nations, was an attempt to rectify the single most sustained crime against humanity: the denial of Jewry's right to its land and its subsequent unparalleled history of suffering.

Winston Churchill never wavered from this view. There were Arab leaders who understood this too. In 1919, King Faisal wrote to the American-Jewish judge Felix Frankfurter: "We Arabs, especially the educated among us, look with the deepest sympathy on the Zionist movement.... The Jewish movement is national and not imperialist. Our movement [Arab nationalism] is national and not imperialist.... Indeed I think that neither can be a real success without the other."

Isn't that, though, exactly what people accuse Israel of being now, an imperialist state?

The idea that Jews came to Israel as outsiders or imperialists is among the most perverse of modern myths. They were the land's original inhabitants; they have the same relationship to the land as native Americans to America, Aborigines to Australia, and Maoris to New Zealand. They were ousted by imperialists. They are the *only* rulers of the land in the past three thousand years who neither sought nor created an empire. In fact, no other people, no other power, has ever created an independent state there. When it was not a Jewish state, Israel was merely an administrative unit of empires: Babylon, Persia, Greece, Rome, and the Christian and Muslim empires between the fourth century and the Ottoman Empire, which lasted until the First World War. The existence of Israel, in ancient times and today, is a sustained protest *against* empires and imperialism.

But do we really need a Jewish state?

There must be some place on earth where Jews can defend themselves, where they have a home in the sense given by the poet Robert Frost, as noted above, as "the place where, when you have to go there, they have to take you in." Every nation has the right to rule itself and create a society and culture in accordance with its own values. That right, to national self-determination, is among the most basic in politics. Today there are eighty-two Christian nations and fifty-six Muslim ones, but only one Jewish one: in a country smaller than the Kruger National Park, one-quarter of one percent of the land mass of the Arab world.

But what about the Palestinians? Surely they too have a right to a state of their own?

They do. Jews long ago recognised this. There were various plans for the partition of the land into two states, one Jewish, one Arab, in the 1920s and 1930s. Jews accepted them; the Arabs rejected them. In 1947, the United Nations voted for partition. Again, Jews accepted, the Arabs refused. David Ben-Gurion reiterated the call for peace as a central part of Israel's Declaration of Independence in May 1948. Israel's neighbours – Egypt, Jordan, Syria, Lebanon, and Iraq – responded by attacking it on all fronts.

The offer was renewed in 1967 after the Six-Day War. The response of the Arab League, meeting in Khartoum in September 1967, was the famous "Three Nos": no to peace, no to negotiations, no to the recognition of the State of Israel. The call was repeated many times by Golda Meir and always decisively rejected.

The boldest offer was made by Ehud Barak at Taba in 2001. It offered the Palestinians a state in the whole of Gaza and 97 percent of the West Bank, with border compensations for the other 3 percent, with East Jerusalem as its capital. The story is told in detail in Dennis Ross' *The Missing Peace* (Ross was the chief US negotiator). Many members of the Palestinian team wanted to accept. The Saudi ambassador at the time, Prince Bandar bin Sultan, said, "If Arafat does not accept what is available now, it won't be a tragedy, it will be a crime."

Tragically, the Palestinians have been betrayed by those who claimed to be their supporters. They were betrayed in 1948 by the Arab states who promised them that if they left now they would return soon, all Jews having been expelled. They were betrayed by the Arab nations to which they fled, who refused to grant them citizenship, in marked contrast to Israel and its treatment of Jewish refugees from Arab (and other) lands.

They were betrayed by countries that encouraged them to pursue violence instead of peace, bringing poverty to an entire population which, under Israeli rule from 1967 to 1987, had achieved unprecedented levels of affluence and economic growth. They are betrayed today by those who encourage impossible expectations – Palestinian rule over the whole of Israel – thus condemning yet another generation to violence, poverty, and despair.

The Egyptians, who ruled Gaza between 1949 and 1967, could have created a Palestinian state, but did not. The Jordanians, who ruled the West Bank during the same years, could have created a Palestinian state, but did not. Instead, Egypt persecuted its Islamist intellectuals, sentencing many to death. The Jordanians expelled the Palestinians in 1971, after killing almost ten thousand of them in 1970 in the massacre known as "Black September." The only country that has ever offered the Palestinians a state is Israel.

What then should be our response to those who criticise Israel?

Criticism of Israel is a legitimate part of democratic politics and free speech. Many of Israel's most acute critics are Israelis. No nation is perfect; no nation can be perfect. A good society is one that makes space for, and listens to, constructive criticism. That is something with which we must live. The Hebrew Bible is the most self-critical document in religious or national history.

What we must challenge are the blatant falsehoods: that Israel is the aggressor, that it has not sought peace; above all the idea that it has no right to exist. Equally we must challenge the false paradigm that the Israel-Palestinian relationship is a zero-sum game in which one side loses and the other wins. It is not. From peace, both sides gain. From war, violence, and terror, both sides lose.

The call on both sides must be for peace: peace for Israel, peace for the Palestinians. You cannot have one without the other. The choice is not between supporting Israel or supporting the Palestinians, but between peace or violence. Peace is sacred, violence a desecration. Too many lives have been lost, too much blood has been shed. Eventually both sides must recognise the other's right to be – and if not now, when?

For further reading

On the formative ideas of Zionism, see:
Arthur Hertzberg, ed., *The Zionist Idea* (1997).

Good histories include:
David Vital, *The Origins of Zionism* (1975),
Martin Gilbert, *Israel: A History* (2008), and
Conor Cruise O'Brien, *The Siege* (1986).

Key documents can be found in:
Walter Laqueur and Barry Rubin, eds., *The Israel-Arab Reader* (2008).

On early non-Jewish support for a Jewish state, see:
Barbara W. Tuchman, *Bible and Sword* (1984).

Making a Difference

Ruth had been silent for a long while. Suddenly she looked up and said, with a sad kind of passion, "I've been listening to everything you've said. But what can we do? The problems are so great and we're so small. What difference can one person make to problems that are deep and global and made by millions of people thinking and acting the way they do?"

Nothing we can do will make a difference. So why try?

Don't believe for one moment that you can't make a difference. It isn't so. Let me tell you a story. Back in the early 1960s, Washington DC was a very racially segregated city. There was a young Black boy, Stephen Carter, who, together with his family, moved into a white neighbourhood. They were among the first Black families to do so.

The first morning he and his brothers and sisters sat on the front step of the house, waiting to see how they would be greeted. They weren't. People ignored them. It was clear that no one wanted them there.

Many years later, Carter wrote about how he felt. "I knew we shouldn't have come here. We aren't welcome. We won't be accepted. We don't belong. We will never belong." In the middle of these thoughts, he was interrupted by the sight of a woman on the other side of the road. She waved at the children, gave them a smile, then disappeared into a house. A few minutes later she reappeared with a tray laden with food and drinks. She brought it over to the children and, still with a smile, told them how pleased she was to see them.

That moment, said Carter, changed my life. Suddenly he realised he could belong. Carter went on to become a professor of law at Yale University and one of America's most distinguished writers on politics. In a book he wrote about the effect of that one act, he spoke about the woman who had made such a difference to his life, who had died tragically young. Her name, he said, was Sarah Kestenbaum. He added (Carter is a Lutheran) that it was no accident that she was religious, and Jewish. Jews, he said, have a name for what she did: *ḥesed,* kindness, especially to strangers, especially when it's hard.

That episode took place in the 1960s. A few years ago I was giving a talk in a Washington synagogue and I happened to tell that story. Someone came up to me afterwards and said that Sarah Kestenbaum used to be a member of this synagogue. "I hadn't heard that story," he added, "but yes, that's the kind of thing Sarah used to do."

One act, one moment, can change a life. Never believe you can't make a difference. You can.

Alright, there can be exceptions. But how often do they happen? And what difference do they really make?

As Jews, we believe that "a single life is like a universe." Change a life and you begin to change the world. In Judaism we believe in the absolute value of the individual. To God we each count, and count separately. Therefore, because problems are made by individuals, they can be solved by individuals. That is where change takes place.

The Rambam, Moses Maimonides, says that we have to act each day as if our lives were evenly poised between good and evil, and as if the world were also evenly poised. Our next act will tilt the balance. Our fate and the fate of the world depend on what we do next. Now it can be hard to think like this all the time. But the Rambam is telling us that we should never think that what we do is insignificant. It isn't. Often we don't realise the impact we have on other people. One kind word, one smile, can give hope to someone on the brink of despair. That, for example, is what I learned from Holocaust survivors.

What would be an example today?

Darfur. What demoralised the victims of the Holocaust was the feeling that the world knew and didn't care. They couldn't understand how a crime of that magnitude could take place without someone, somewhere, doing something. That, more than anything else, made them feel abandoned and alone.

A slow genocide is taking place in Darfur and we have to protest. Protests make a difference. Public awareness grows.

Politicians ask questions. Television documentaries get made. International pressure mounts. Governments back down. It takes time, hard work, effort, and commitment, but eventually others take up the cause and things happen.

One campaign, started by Jewish students in Britain, brought about one of the most remarkable developments in recent political history. After the Six-Day War in 1967, many Russian Jews wanted to go to Israel. Russia under communist rule was hostile to Israel. The Jews who wanted to leave found themselves losing their jobs and subjected to harassment. In some cases – most famously Natan Sharansky – they were imprisoned. They were known as "refuseniks."

Jewish students in Britain took up their cause: it was called the Soviet Jewry Campaign. Eventually it spread to the United States. Jews throughout America became involved. Bar and bat mitzvas were twinned with Jewish children in Russia. People handed out leaflets in their neighbourhoods, explaining the refuseniks' plight. Rallies were organised. Leading senators and congressmen were enlisted.

Eventually more than a million Jews were enabled to leave Russia and go to Israel: 200,000 in the 1970s, the rest in the 1990s. It was one of the most successful campaigns in modern history and had a huge effect on both Israel and Russia. I was a student when the campaign began. I saw how a handful of Jewish students started a process that became a snowball and then an avalanche. If I ever doubted that individuals can make a difference, that campaign convinced me otherwise.

So what is your message to Jewish students today?

There is a story that had a major impact on me. In the summer of 1968 a British Jewish student spent his vacation in America. The weeks leading up to the Six-Day War, when it seemed as if Israel might be facing destruction, had shaken him. Besides which, he was studying philosophy, and in those days philosophers took a dim view of religion. He had many questions about Jewish identity and faith, and he wanted to discuss them with people who had thought them through.

He knew there were distinguished Jewish thinkers in America, so the next summer he went there, bought a Greyhound bus ticket and travelled from city to city, tracking down the great rabbis mentioned in a survey he had read in an American Jewish journal. They all had interesting things to say, but many of them mentioned the name of the man they thought was the greatest rabbi of the time, the Lubavitcher Rebbe.

So the student travelled to the Rebbe's headquarters in Brooklyn. He told people there that he wanted to see the great man. They laughed. There are thousands of people who want to see the Rebbe, they said. It will take months to organise a meeting. The student asked them to ask the Rebbe nonetheless, and left them phone numbers and addresses where they could contact him.

Eventually the call came through one Sunday night: the Rebbe can see you on Thursday. The student travelled non-stop for three days on a bus from Los Angeles to New York, and eventually found himself in the Rebbe's office. He asked the Rebbe his questions. The Rebbe answered them. Then the Rebbe turned the conversation around. "What are you doing" he asked, "for Jewish students at your university?" The student was disoriented. He wasn't a leader. He wasn't particularly involved. But the Rebbe kept challenging him, telling him he could make a difference.

The student returned to university, but the Rebbe's challenge stayed in his mind. He had never intended to get involved in Jewish life, beyond turning up. But someone had given him a task, and it kept beating at the door of his consciousness. Eventually the student did get involved. He became president of the university Jewish society. Several years later he trained to become a rabbi. Later still he became a chief rabbi. I was that student.

I became a leader not because I wanted to but because someone made me realise that the Jewish future depended on us – on me and the members of my generation. And I made myself the promise that one day I would challenge Jewish students the way the Rebbe had challenged me. I am not a rebbe; but the Jewish future depends on you.

There are huge challenges, some negative like antisemitism and anti-Zionism, but most of them positive: reaching out to other Jewish students and helping make Judaism speak to a new generation, fighting for the people of Darfur, working with people of other faiths to create a more tolerant society, getting involved in social action projects in Britain, or helping to fight poverty and disease in Third World countries.

Never believe you can't make a difference. You can.

For further reading

My own book on this subject is *To Heal a Fractured World* (2007).

See also:
Warren Goldstein, *Defending the Human Spirit* (2005), Joseph Telushkin, *The Book of Jewish Values* (2000), and Elliot Dorff, *The Way into Tikkun Olam (Repairing the World)* (2007).

READINGS

This section offers a collection of original writings and collated texts that formed the booklet *Ten Days, Ten Ways: Paths to the Divine Presence*, which was originally published in September 2007. This booklet was designed to inspire and to prepare readers for the High Holy Days. Rosh HaShana, Yom Kippur, and the days between are the time when we come closest to God – reflecting on our life, our purpose, our identity. Here you can find a selection of texts written and carefully chosen by Rabbi Sacks as starting points for personal reflection and meditation, ten paths leading to a more fulfilled and spiritual life.

INTRODUCTION TO TEN DAYS, TEN WAYS: PATHS TO THE DIVINE PRESENCE

"Seek God where He is to be found, call Him when He is close." The Sages were puzzled by this verse. *When is God not close? Surely God is everywhere. Their answer was profound. God is always close to us, but we are not always close to God.* When are we close? "During the ten days between Rosh HaShana and Yom Kippur."

Why is God close on these days? Because it is then, when asking to be written in the Book of Life, that we reflect most deeply on our own life. What have I achieved? What have I failed to achieve? What did I do wrong? How can I put it right? What am I here to do?

Whether we believe, or don't believe, these are religious questions. Science can tell us how life began, but it can never tell us what life is for. Anthropology can tell us the many ways in which people have lived, but it can never tell us how we should live. Economics and business studies can tell us how to generate wealth, but they cannot tell us what to do with the wealth we have made.

The various sciences, natural, social or human, can tell us how, but not why. The "why" questions ask us to lift up our eyes beyond the immediate, in search of the ultimate. The name we give to the ultimate is God. The search for meaning is the religious quest, and on Rosh HaShana and Yom Kippur it reaches its greatest intensity.

God is always close to us, but we are not always close to God. How then do we come close to Him? By living Jewishly. "We will do, then we will understand," said our ancestors at Mount Sinai. So it is in all matters of the soul. We learn to love music by listening to music. We learn to be generous by performing acts of generosity. "The heart follows the deed." Don't expect to have faith or find God by waiting for Him to find us. We have to begin the journey. Then God meets us halfway.

There are many ways of finding God, many paths to the Divine Presence. In this anthology I have chosen ten of the most important, one for each of the days from the start of Rosh HaShana to the end of Yom Kippur. The first is *identity*. We are born into a family that has a history. Who are we? To which story do we belong?

The second is *prayer*, the most focused way in which we reach out to God. Third is *study*, the highest of all Jewish acts, which the Sages said was more holy even than prayer.

Fourth is *mitzvot*, the way of the commands. In prayer we find God by speaking; in study we find God in listening; in mitzvot we find God by doing.

Then come the three great attributes of the Jewish personality: *tzedaka*, love as justice; *ḥesed*, love as compassion; and *emuna*, love as loyalty. Judaism is a religion of love, not the mystical, otherworldly love that hovers above the world, leaving its imperfections intact, but the love that engages with the world, trying – one act at a time, one day at a time, one life at a time – to make it a little less cruel, a little more human and humane.

Then, lastly, come the three great expressions of Jewish life: *Israel*, the one place on earth where Jews have the chance to do what every other nation takes for granted, namely, the right to rule ourselves and create a society in accordance with our beliefs; *kiddush Hashem*, sanctifying God's name in the world by acting as God's ambassadors; and lastly *Jewish responsibility*, the idea that we are God's partners in the work of creation, and there is work for each of us to do in this tense and troubled age.

This is not a sequential book; it is an anthology of readings, any of which may be the starting point of a personal meditation, framed by such questions as: How does this apply to me? How can I act on it in the year to come? Some may not speak to you, others will. For there are as many ways to the Divine Presence as there are Jews, said Rav Nahman of Breslov. Or as I put it: Where *what we want to do* meets *what needs to be done*, that is where God wants us to be.

There are many ways to God. Where we begin doesn't matter, so long as we begin. Jewish life is the circumference of a circle at whose centre is God. That is where we meet, whatever our starting point.

However long we live, life is short, too short. Every day matters. Every day in which we do not do some good deed, take some step towards God, make some difference to the world, is a day wasted – and our days on earth are too few to waste even one. May God bless you in the coming year, and may He bless us all, with peace, with health, with happiness, with life.

Jonathan Sacks
Tishrei 5768

1. The Way of Identity: On Being a Jew

Uniquely, Jews are born into a faith. It chooses us before we choose it. Physically we come naked into the world, but spiritually we come with a gift: the story of our past, of our parents and theirs through forty centuries from the day Abraham and Sarah first heard the call of God and began their journey to a land, a promise, a destiny, and a vocation. That story is ours.

It is a strange and moving story. It tells of how a family, then a collection of tribes, then a nation, were summoned to be God's ambassadors on earth. They were charged with building a society unlike any other, based not on wealth or power but on justice and compassion, the dignity of the individual and the sanctity of human life – a society that would honour the world as God's work and the human person as God's image.

This was and is a demanding task, yet Judaism remains a realistic religion. It assumed from the outset that transforming the world would take many generations – hence the importance of handing on our ideals to the next generation. It takes many gifts, many different kinds of talent – hence the importance of Jews as a people. None of us has all the gifts but each of us has some. We all count; we each have a unique contribution to make. We come before God as a people, each giving something, each lifted by the contributions of others.

And yes, at times we fail or fall short – hence the importance of *teshuva*, repentance, apology, forgiveness, rededication. Judaism is bigger than any of us, yet it is made by all of us. And though Jews were and are a tiny people, today a mere fifth of a percent of the population of the world, we have made a contribution to civilisation out of all proportion to our numbers.

Who are we, and what are we called on to do?

Genesis: The Call

The Lord said to Abram, "Go – from your land, your birthplace, and your father's house – to the land that I will show you. I will make you a great nation, and I will bless you and make your name great. You will become a blessing. And I will bless those who bless you, and those who curse you I will curse. And through you, all the families of the earth will be blessed."

Genesis 12:1–3

Genesis: The Way of the Lord

Abraham is about to become a great and mighty nation, and through him all the nations on earth will be blessed. For I have chosen him so that he may direct his children and his household after him to keep the way of the Lord by doing what is right and just, that the Lord may bring about for Abraham what He spoke of for him.

Genesis 18:18–19

The Covenant at Sinai: A Holy Nation

You yourselves have seen what I did to the Egyptians: how I lifted you up on eagles' wings and brought you to Me. Now, if you faithfully heed My voice and keep My covenant, you will be My treasure among all the peoples, although the whole earth is Mine. A kingdom of priests and a holy nation you shall be to Me.

Exodus 19:4–6

Moses: A People of History

Ask now about earliest times, times long before your own, from the day God created humans on the earth; ask from one end of heaven to the other: Has anything as great as this ever happened before? Has anyone heard of anything like this? Has any people ever heard the voice of God speaking out of fire, as you have, and lived? Has God ever taken one nation to Himself, by miracles, from the midst of another, by trials, signs, wonders, and war, with a mighty hand and an arm stretched forth and terrifying displays of power, as the Lord your God did for you in Egypt before your eyes?

Deuteronomy 4:32–34

Isaiah: A Light to the Nations

I, the Lord, call you forth in victory, and I will hold your hand; I shall form you and make you a covenant people, make you a light unto nations, to open blinded eyes, to bring prisoners out of captivity, and those who dwell in darkness from their jail.

Isaiah 42:6–7

Dust and the Stars

"I will multiply your seed like the stars of the heaven and the sand on the seashore" (Gen. 22:17). R. Yehuda bar Ilai explained: This people is compared to dust and to the stars. When it sinks, it sinks to the dust, but when it rises, it rises to the stars.

"I will make your offspring like the dust of the earth" (Gen. 13:16). As the dust of the earth is from one end of the world to the other, so your children will be dispersed from one end of the world to the other. As dust is trodden on by all, so will your children be trodden on by the peoples of the world. As dust outlives all vessels of metal while it endures forever, so all the peoples of the earth will cease to be, while Israel endures forever.

Megilla 16a

Like Fragrant Oil

"Your name is like fragrant oil poured out" (Song. 1:3): As oil brings light to the world, so Israel brings light to the world, as it is said, "Nations will come to your light, and kings to the brightness of your dawn" (Is. 60:3).

Song of Songs Rabba 1:3:2

Saadia Gaon

Our nation is a nation only in virtue of its Torah.

Emunot VeDeot (The Book of Beliefs and Opinions) 3:7

Judah HaLevi

Israel is to the nations as the heart is to the limbs of the body.

Kuzari, II:36

Loyalty to God

Devoid of power, splendour, bereft of the brilliant show of human grandeur, Israel was upheld by its faithfulness towards the All-One.... Other states, everywhere, in all the glory of human power and arrogance, disappeared from the face of the earth, while Israel, though devoid of might and splendour, lived on because of its loyalty to God and His Law.

Rabbi Samson Raphael Hirsch, *The Nineteen Letters,* 64

Hope in Failure

Despair and resignation were unknown to the man of the covenant who found triumph in defeat, hope in failure, and who could not conceal God's Word that was, to paraphrase Jeremiah, deeply implanted in his bones and burning in his heart like an all-consuming fire.

Rabbi Joseph Soloveitchik, *The Lonely Man of Faith,* 112

The Ennoblement of the Human Race

The pursuit of knowledge for its own sake, an almost fanatical love of justice, and the desire for personal independence – these are the features of the Jewish tradition which make me thank my stars that I belong to it.

Albert Einstein, *As I See It*, 103

Bigger Than Our Numbers

Each of us Jews knows how thoroughly ordinary he is; yet taken together, we seem caught up in things great and inexplicable.... The number of Jews in the world is smaller than a small statistical error in the Chinese census. Yet we remain bigger than our numbers. Big things seem to happen around us and to us.

Milton Himmelfarb, *Jews and Gentiles*, 141–42

Looking Outward

We have become altogether too inward-looking, with our horizons largely limited within the ghetto-walls we have erected to separate us from the rest of our people and from the human society beyond.... Preoccupied with the burning problems of our own survival, we have lost sight with our assignment as a light unto the nations.

Lord Jakobovits, *The Timely and the Timeless*, 96–97

Remaking the World

For forty centuries, Jews have held tenaciously to the belief that we have been charged with a sacred mission: to sanctify life by being God's ambassadors to a world that has all too often worshipped the multiple forms of what Nietzsche called "the will to power." We were called on to write a different story, that tells of the beauty of holiness and the call of compassion: "to tame the savageness of man and make gentle the life of this world."

Judaism has placed at the centre of its striving some of the most healing of all sacred imperatives: the importance of love and loyalty; marriage and the sacred bonds between husband and wife, parent and child; education and the life of the mind; justice, equity, and the rule of law; compassion, charity, and human dignity; the bonds of belonging and community; memory, history, and imperishable hope. We seek God not just in the remote heavens or the innermost recesses of the soul but in ordinary life, with its pleasures and pains, fears and hopes, conflicts and consolations. Judaism believes not in abandoning earth for the sake of heaven, but in bringing fragments of heaven down to earth in simple deeds and celebrations.

For that is where God is found. Not in wealth, power, fame, success, or any other of the myriad substitutes for life, still less in violence and terror, but in life itself: living, breathing (*neshama,* the Hebrew word for soul, means "breathing"), loving, giving, caring, praying, praising, giving thanks, defeating tragedy in the name of hope, and death in the name of life.

Our task is to be true to our faith and a blessing to others: a blessing to others *because* we are true to our faith. To be a Jew is to bring redemption, one day at a time, one act at a time. Every mitzva, every kind word or deed, every act of sharing what we have with others, brings the Divine Presence into the world. By recognising the image of God in other people, we help to remake the world in the image of God.

Jonathan Sacks

Prayer

Ribbono shel Olam, Sovereign of the Universe, help me live my people's destiny, as an heir to the covenant our ancestors made with You at Sinai. May I honour our people's past and help build our people's future.

2. The Way of Prayer: Speaking to God

Prayer is our intimate dialogue with Infinity, the profoundest expression of our faith that at the heart of reality is a Presence that cares, a God who listens, a creative Force that brought us into being in love. It is this belief more than any other that redeems life from solitude and fate from tragedy. The universe has a purpose. We have a purpose. However infinitesimal we are, however brief our stay on earth, we matter. The universe is more than particles of matter endlessly revolving in indifferent space. The human person is more than an accidental concatenation of genes blindly replicating themselves. Human life is more than "a tale, told by an idiot, full of sound and fury, signifying nothing." Prayer gives meaning to existence.

It is possible to believe otherwise. There can be a life without faith or prayer, just as there can be a life without love, or laughter, or happiness, or hope. But it is a diminished thing, lacking dimensions of depth and aspiration. Descartes said, "I think, therefore I am." Judaism says, "I pray, therefore I am not alone."

It takes courage to believe. Jews need no proof of the apparent injustice of events. It is written on the pages of our history. Jews had no power or earthly glory. For the better part of forty centuries our ancestors lived dispersed throughout the world, without a home, without rights, all too often experiencing persecution and pain. All they had was an invisible God and the line connecting us to Him: the siddur, the words of prayer. All they had was faith. And in Judaism, we do not analyse our faith; we pray it. We do not philosophise about truth: we sing it, *daven* it. For Judaism, faith becomes real when it becomes prayer.

In prayer we speak to a presence vaster than the unfathomable universe yet closer to us than we are to ourselves: the God beyond who is also the Voice within. Though language must fail when we try to describe a Being beyond all parameters of speech, yet language is all we have, and it is enough. For God who made the world with creative words, and who revealed His will in holy words, listens to our prayerful words. Language is the bridge that joins us to Infinity.

In prayer God becomes not a theory but a Presence, not a fact but a mode of relationship. Prayer is where God meets us, in the human heart, in our offering of words, in our acknowledged vulnerability.

R. Elazar's Prayer: Love and Fellowship

May it be Your will, O Lord our God, to cause to dwell in our lot
love, fellowship, peace, and friendship,
to widen our boundaries through disciples,
to prosper our goal with hope and with future, to appoint us a share in the Garden of Eden,
to direct us in Your world
through good companions and good impulse, that we may rise in the morning and find our heart awake to fear Your name.

Berakhot 16b

Rabbi Judah HaLevi: Where Shall I Find You?

Lord, where shall I find You?
High and hidden is Your place.
And where shall I not find You?
Your glory fills infinities of space…
I have sought Your presence,
called You with all my heart.
And going out to meet You
I found You coming toward me.

From a poem by Judah HaLevi, *Selected Poems of Jehudah Halevi,* 134

Rabbi Shlomo ibn Gabirol: Before I Was Born

Before I was born, Your love enveloped me.
You turned nothing into substance, and created me.
Who etched out my frame? Who poured
me into a vessel and moulded me?
Who breathed a spirit into me? Who opened
the womb of Sheol and extracted me?
Who has guided me from youth-time until now?
Taught me knowledge, and cared wondrously for me?
Truly, I am nothing but clay within Your hand.
It is You, not I, who have really fashioned me.
I confess my sin to You, and do not say
that a serpent intrigued, and tempted me.
How can I conceal from You my faults, since
before I was born Your love enveloped me?

Rabbi Shlomo ibn Gabirol, "Before I was Born,"
in David Goldstein, *The Jewish Poets of Spain*, 97

Rabbi Elazar Azikri: In My Heart I Will Build a Sanctuary

In my heart I will build a sanctuary
To God's glorious splendour.
And in the sanctuary I will raise an altar
to the radiance of His majesty.
As fire I will take
the fire of the Binding,
and as a sacrifice I will offer Him
my undivided soul.

Adapted from Rabbi Elazar Azikri, *Sefer Ḥaredim*

Lord and King of Peace

Lord and King of peace,
who makes peace and creates all things:
Help all of us that we may always hold fast to the attribute of peace,
so that true and abundant peace prevail between man and man, between husband and wife.
And no strife separate humankind even in thought.
You make peace in Your heaven,
You bring contrary elements together:
Extend abundant peace to us and to the whole world,
so that all discords be resolved in great love and peace.
And with one mind, one heart, all come near to You and Your law in truth,
and all form one union to do Your will with a whole heart.
Lord of peace, bless us with peace.

Rabbi Nahman of Breslov, *Likkutei Tefillot,* I, 95

The Music of Prayer

There are people who cannot understand prayer and its effect on the soul. The Baal Shem Tov explained this by way of a parable. He said: There was once a musician who played so beautifully that those who heard him stopped and began to dance. Once a deaf man came along. He saw all the people dancing but he could not hear the music. He thought they were all mad.

Work and Prayer

Rabbi Nahman of Kosov taught that we should always have God in our thoughts. "But how," asked a disciple, "can we think of God while we are engaged in business?" The rabbi replied: "If we can think of business when we are praying, then we can think of praying when we are doing business."

Welcome Back

Once Rabbi Levi Yitzhak of Berdichev walked over to a group of his disciples after prayers had ended and welcomed them: "*Shalom aleikhem.*" The disciples were surprised and asked the Rebbe what he meant. They hadn't been away. "I was speaking," he said, "not to your bodies but your minds. I saw that while you were praying, you were thinking about other things. Your bodies were here but your minds were far away. Now that they have returned, I wished them *Shalom aleikhem.*"

Inspiration

One day some American visitors came to the synagogue in Shaarei Ḥesed, Jerusalem, where the great sage Rabbi Shlomo Zalman Auerbach prayed. Their nine-year-old son, standing behind Rabbi Auerbach, said the *Amida* so slowly and intently that the rabbi was unable to take three steps backward until the boy was finished. After the service the father apologised to the rabbi for the inconvenience. "On the contrary," said

Rabbi Shlomo Zalman, "I would like to thank your son for the inspiration of his devotion."

Adapted from Hanoch Teller,
And from Jerusalem His Word, 256–57

At One with Creation

All beings long for the very source of their origin. Every plant, every grain of sand, every clod of earth, small creatures and great, the heavens and the angels, every substance and its particles – all of them are longing, yearning, panting to attain the state of holy perfection. Human beings suffer constantly from this homesickness of the soul, and it is in prayer that we cure it. When praying, we feel at one with the whole creation, and raise it to the very source of blessing and life.

Rabbi Avraham Kook, *Olat Re'aya,*
Commentary on the Siddur

Is Prayer Answered?

Is prayer answered? If God is changeless, how can we change Him by what we say? Even discounting this, why do we need to articulate our requests? Surely God, who sees the heart, knows our wishes even before we do, without our having to put them into words. What we wish to happen is either right or wrong in the eyes of God. If it is right, God will bring it about even if we do not pray. If it is wrong, God will not bring it about even if we do. So why pray?

The classic Jewish answer is simple but profound. Without a vessel to contain a blessing, there can be no blessing. If we have no receptacle to catch the rain, the rain may fall, but we will have none to drink. If we have no radio receiver, the sound waves will flow, but we will be unable to convert them into sound. God's blessings flow continuously, but unless we make ourselves into a vessel for them, they will flow elsewhere. Prayer is the act of turning ourselves into a vehicle for the Divine. Prayer changes the world because it changes us.

Jonathan Sacks, introduction to the *Authorised Daily Prayer Book,* also published as the *Koren Shalem Siddur*

Prayer

Ribbono shel Olam, Sovereign of the Universe, help me pray from the heart. Hear my words, my thanks, my hopes, my fears. Teach me to speak honestly and to listen attentively.

3. The Way of Study: Listening to God

Jews are the people of the book. *Talmud Torah* – studying Torah – is the greatest of all the commands and the secret of Jewish continuity. In the *Shema* we are commanded, "Love the Lord your God with all your heart, your soul, and your might." Then almost immediately it says, "Teach these things repeatedly to your children, speaking of them when you sit at home and when you travel on the way, when you lie down and when you rise." Judaism is a religion of education.

Study is holier even than prayer, for in prayer we speak to God, but in study we listen to God. We strive to understand what God wants from us. We try to make His will ours. For the holiest thing is God's word. The Torah – God's word to our ancestors – is our constitution as a nation, our covenant of liberty, the code by which we decipher the mystery and meaning of life.

The words of the Torah span a thousand years, from Moses to Malachi, the first and last of the prophets. For another thousand years, until the completion of the Babylonian Talmud, Jews added commentaries to the book, and for another thousand years they wrote commentaries to the commentaries. Never has there been a deeper relationship between a people and a book. The ancient Greeks, puzzled by the phenomenon of an entire people dedicated to learning, called Jews "a nation of philosophers." Certainly we are called on to be a nation of students and teachers. In Judaism we not only learn to live; we live to learn. In study, we make Torah real in the mind so that we can make it actual in the world.

How I Love Your Teaching

How I love Your teaching!
All day long I reflect upon it.
How sweet Your promise is to my palate,
sweeter than honey to my mouth!
Your word is a lamp for my feet,
a light for my path.
Your decrees are my everlasting share,
for they are the joy of my heart.
Your words shine light as they unfold,
granting insight to the simple.
Your decrees are ever just;
grant me insight, and I will live.

Psalms 119:97, 103, 105, 111, 130, 144

Your Children's Peace

All your children will be students of the Lord,
and great will be your children's peace.

Isaiah 54:13

The Testimony of Josephus

Should any one of our nation be asked about our laws, he will repeat them as readily as his own name. The result of our thorough education in our laws from the very dawn of intelligence is that they are, as it were, engraved on our souls.

Josephus, *Contra Apionem*, II, 177–78

The World's First Universal Education System

H. G. Wells noted in his Outline of History that "the Jewish religion, because it was a literature-sustained religion, led to the first efforts to provide elementary education for all children in the community." Universal compulsory education did not exist in England until 1870; it existed in Israel eighteen centuries earlier. This talmudic passage gives a thumbnail history of how it evolved.

May the name of Yehoshua ben Gamla be remembered for good, for were it not for him, the Torah would have been forgotten from Israel. For at first if a child had a father, his father taught him, and if he had no father he did not learn at all. Then they made an ordinance that teachers of children should be appointed in Jerusalem. Even then, however, if a child had a father, the father would take him to Jerusalem to have him taught, but if not, the child would not go. They then ordained that teachers should be appointed in every district, and boys would enter school at the age of sixteen or seventeen. But then, if the teacher punished a child, the child would rebel and leave school. Eventually Yehoshua ben Gamla came and ordained that teachers of young children should be appointed in each district and town, and that children should enter school at the age of six or seven.

Abridged from Bava Batra 21a

The Three Crowns

With three crowns was Israel crowned – with the crown of the Torah, the crown of the priesthood, and the crown of sovereignty. The crown of the priesthood was bestowed on Aaron.… The crown of sovereignty was conferred on David.… But the crown of the Torah is for all Israel, as it is said, "Moses commanded us a law, an inheritance of the congregation of Jacob" (Deut. 33:4). Whoever desires it can win it. Do not suppose that the other two crowns are greater than the crown of the Torah, for it is said, "By me, kings reign and princes decree justice. By me, princes rule" (Prov. 8:15–16). Hence you can infer that the crown of the Torah is greater than the other two crowns.

Maimonides, *Mishneh Torah, Hilkhot Talmud Torah* 3:1

Non-Jewish Testimony

A twelfth-century Christian monk wrote the following in one of his commentaries, in an age in which most of Europe was illiterate:

The Jews, out of their zeal for God and their love of the Law, put as many sons as they have to letters, that each may understand God's Law.... A Jew, however poor, if he had ten sons, would put them all to letters, not for gain, as the Christians do, but for the understanding of God's Law; and not only his sons but his daughters.

B. Smalley, *The Study of the Bible in the Middle Ages*, 78

The Medieval Custom: A Child's First Day at School

This beautiful ceremony tells us how Jews in the Middle Ages celebrated a young child's first day at school. The rabbi and community leaders would join the celebration, and they would say that bringing a child to school is "as though they had brought him to Mount Sinai."

They write the letters of the Hebrew alphabet on a board for him; and they wash him and dress him in clean garments, and they knead him three loaves of fine wheat in honey.... And they boil him three eggs and bring him apples and other kinds of fruit, and seek a worthy sage to conduct him to the schoolhouse. He covers him with his prayer-shawl and brings him to the synagogue, where they feed him with loaves of honey and eggs and fruit; and they read him the letters. After that they cover the board with honey and tell him to lick it. Then they lead him back to his mother.

Maḥzor Vitri, para. 508

Jewish Education in the Shtetl

From infancy the boy is guided and prodded towards scholarship. In the cradle he will listen to his mother's lullabies: "Sleep soundly at night and learn Torah by day / And thou'lt be a Rabbi when I have grown grey."

The most important item in the family budget is the tuition fee that must be paid each term to the teacher of the younger boy's school. "Parents will bend the sky to educate their son." The mother, who has charge of household accounts, will cut the family food costs to the limit if necessary, in order to pay for her sons' schooling. If the worst comes to the worst, she will pawn her cherished pearls in order to pay for the school term. The boy must study, the boy must become a good Jew – for her, the two are synonymous.

Mark Zborowski and Elizabeth Herzog,
Life Is with People, 85–87

Communities Built Around Schools

The history of the Jews has been a history of communities built around schools. They are the key institutions because they convey learning. Greek civilization survived for five hundred years after the Roman conquest of the Greek city-states, because the Greeks, like the Jews, had developed academies and they could live around those academies. When the academies failed, Greek civilization disappeared. The Jewish people has never allowed its academies to fail.

Daniel J. Elazar, *People and Polity,* 489

Learning Makes Sweet

Rabbi Shlomo Zalman Auerbach said: "For one who learns Torah, even if he only has an onion to eat, it becomes a sweet onion."

Hanoch Teller, *And from Jerusalem His Word,* 72

The Secret of Jewish Continuity

The Israelites, slaves in Egypt for more than two hundred years, were about to go free. On the brink of their release Moses, the leader of the Jews, gathered them together and prepared to address them. He spoke not about freedom, or the promised land, or the journey across the wilderness that lay ahead. Instead he spoke about children and the distant future, and the duty to pass on memory to generations yet unborn. About to gain their freedom, the Israelites were told that they had to become a nation of educators.

Freedom, Moses intimated, is won not on the battlefield, nor in the political arena, but in the human imagination and will. To defend a land you need an army. But to defend freedom you need education. You need families and schools to ensure that your ideals are passed on to the next generation, and never lost, or despaired of, or obscured. So Judaism became a religion of education. Its citadels are houses of study, its heroes teachers, and its passion, study and the life of the mind. Jews achieved immortality not by building monuments or mausoleums – but by engraving their values on the hearts of their children, and they on theirs, and so on until the end of time.

The Israelites built living monuments – monuments to life – and became a people dedicated to bringing new generations into being, and handing on to them the heritage of the past. Their great institutions were the family and education via the conversation between the generations. In place of temples they built houses of prayer and study. In place of stones they had words and teachings. In that counterintuitive reversal they discovered the secret of eternity.

Jonathan Sacks, *Radical Then, Radical Now,* ch. 3

Prayer

Ribbono shel Olam, Sovereign of the Universe, help me to learn more in the coming year. Open my heart to Your Torah, my mind to its teachings, my spirit to its inspiration. Help me to learn from others, to teach others, and to live what I learn and teach.

4. The Way of Mitzvot: Responding to God

Judaism's genius was to take high ideals and translate them into life by simple daily deeds: the way of mitzvot, acting in accordance with God's will. We do not just contemplate truth; we live it.

We don't contemplate creation by studying theoretical physics. We live it by making a blessing over what we eat and drink, acknowledging God as the creator of all we enjoy. We don't think about our responsibility for the environment. We keep Shabbat, setting a limit, one day in seven, to our exploitation of the world. We don't just study Jewish history. On the fasts and festivals, we reenact it. Truth becomes real when it becomes deed. That is how we transform the world.

There are those who see the world as it is and accept it. That is the stoic way. There are those who see the world as it is and flee from it. That is the mystic, monastic way. But there are those who see the world as it is and change it. That is the Jewish way. We change it through mitzvot, holy deeds that bring a fragment of heaven down to earth.

Every mitzva is a miniature act of redemption. It turns something secular into something holy. When we keep *kashrut* we turn food for the body into sustenance for the soul. When we keep Shabbat we sanctify time, making space in our life to breathe and give thanks, celebrating what we have instead of striving for what we do not yet have. When we observe the festivals we sanctify history by turning it into personal memory, forging a connection between our ancestors' past and our present. When we keep the laws of *taharat hamishpaḥa,* family purity, we turn a physical relationship into a sacred bond of love.

The mitzvot bring God into our lives through the intricate choreography of a life lived in accordance with God's will. They are the poetry of the everyday, turning life into a sacred work of art.

Mitzvot teach us that faith is active, not passive. It is a matter of what we do, not just what happens to us. Performing a mitzva, we come close to God, becoming His "partner in the work of creation." Every mitzva is a window in the wall separating us from God. Each mitzva lets God's light flow into the world.

Loving the Law

I rejoice in following Your decrees
as if in great wealth.
I am but a stranger on earth –
do not hide Your commandments from me.

My soul is shattered with longing
at all times for Your laws.
Yes, Your statutes are my delight;
they are my advisors.
Teach me the ways of Your statutes, Lord,
and I will keep to them to the end.
Grant me insight to keep Your teaching,
and I will uphold it with all my heart.
I will walk about freely,
for I seek out Your precepts.
I speak of Your decrees in the presence of kings
without shame.

Psalms 119:14, 19–20, 24, 33–34, 45–46

Our Life and the Length of Our Days

With everlasting love have You loved Your people, the House of Israel. You have taught us Torah and commands, decrees and laws of justice. Therefore, Lord our God, when we lie down and when we rise up we will speak of Your decrees, rejoicing in the words of Your Torah and Your commands for ever. For they are our life and the length of our days; on them will we meditate day and night.

Authorised Daily Prayer Book, 204–5
also published as the *Koren Shalem Siddur*

Every Mitzva Is a Step on the Path to Perfection

If we could only fathom the inner meaning of the commands, we would realise that the essence of the

Torah lies in the deeper meaning of its positive and negative precepts, each one of which aids us in our striving after perfection, removing the impediments to the attainment of excellence.

Maimonides, *The Epistle to Yemen*

Israel's Faithfulness to the Commands

The hasidic master Rabbi Levi Yitzhak of Berdichev always sought to see the merits of his fellow Jews, not their faults. He became his people's advocate before God, their counsel for the defence. This he did one year in a remarkable way.

At that time, the political relationship between Russia and Turkey was hostile. All Turkish merchandise was considered contraband in Russia. The penalty for possession of Turkish goods ranged from long imprisonment to death.

One Passover night before the Seder, the Berdichever told his congregation that he could not begin the Seder without some Turkish snuff, and ordered them to find some Turkish snuff for him.

"But Rebbe," the followers responded, "you know that Turkish tobacco is forbidden. No one would risk the punishment for possessing Turkish snuff."

"No matter," the Rebbe answered. "I must have Turkish snuff."

The people dispersed, and before long brought the Rebbe some Turkish snuff which someone had concealed.

"Good," said the Rebbe, "now I must have some fine Turkish wool. I want a bolt of woollen cloth from Turkey."

"An impossible request," the people said. "No one is foolish enough to own Turkish material today."

"Then there shall be no Seder," the Berdichever said. "We do not begin the Seder unless you bring the Turkish wool."

Again the crowd dispersed, and eventually brought the contraband wool to the Rebbe.

"Good," the Rebbe said. "Now bring me a piece of bread from a Jewish home."

"But Rebbe," the followers answered, "tonight is Passover. There is no bread in any Jewish home."

"Never mind," said the Rebbe. "You searched until you found other contraband. Go search for the bread."

After an extensive search, the people returned empty-handed. Nowhere in Berdichev was there to be found a Jewish household that had a morsel of bread.

The Berdichever lifted his eyes towards heaven. "Look, *Ribbono shel Olam,* Sovereign of the Universe! The czar has a mighty army and well-armed police who are permitted to shoot on sight anyone who defies his laws. He has ordered that under penalty of death, no one dare possess any Turkish goods. Yet when I wanted Turkish snuff, it was to be had. I wanted Turkish wool, and it too was to be found. But You, dear God, You do not have an army. No one fears that he will be shot on sight or imprisoned. Yet You have said that no one is to have *ḥametz* in their possession tonight, and not a single crumb can be found in a Jewish home. Their love and devotion for You far exceeds the fear of mortal punishment. Tell me, *Ribbono shel Olam,* with such devotion from Your children, do they not deserve better treatment than You have been according them?"

Adapted from Abraham J. Twerski,
Generation to Generation, 160–61

The Commandments: Not Truth Thought but Truth Lived

Mitzvot mark a fundamental difference between Judaism, the life of faith, and the civilisation of ancient Greece and its supreme expression, philosophy. Philosophy represents truth thought; Judaism represents truth lived. The Greeks sought knowledge of what is. Jews sought knowledge of what ought to be. So, though Judaism is a set of beliefs, it is not a creed. Instead it is a series of truths that only become true in virtue of the fact that we have lived them. By living them we turn the "ought" into the "is." We make a fragment of perfection in an imperfect world and create a living truth, a life of faith. By keeping mitzvot, following the commandments, we help transform the world that is into the world that ought to be.

The great principles of Jewish faith are creation, revelation, and redemption. But these are not truths we discover; they are truths we make real by living them. On Shabbat we live creation. Learning Torah we live revelation. Performing acts of *ḥesed* and *tzedaka,* we live redemption. We do not philosophise about these things; we enact them. Judaism is not faith thought but faith lived.

No unified field theory will ever finally settle the question of whether or not the universe was created by a personal God. No historical investigation will ever resolve the question of whether, at Sinai, the voice the Israelites heard was real or imagined. No political theory will ever determine whether or not a just and compassionate society is possible. That is not because these things are irrational. It is because they represent truths that can only be made real in life.

I can believe that love exists, or I can believe that it is an illusion. Both views are coherent. I must choose, and that choice will shape my life, leading me to marry or to stay aloof, perhaps having "relationships" but not a total commitment to another person. Believing in love, I find it.

Disbelieving it, I never experience it. Faith is neither rational nor irrational. It is the courage to turn "ought" into "is." It is the willingness to listen to the commanding, summoning voice and turn it into deed. Mitzvot are ideals made real in the doing. The great truths of the human situation must be lived.

Jonathan Sacks, *Radical Then, Radical Now*, ch. 12

Prayer

Ribbono shel Olam, Sovereign of the Universe, help me to keep more mitzvot in the coming year. Teach me to act as You would wish me to act, that I may become an agent of Your will in the world.

5. The Way of *Tzedaka*: Love as Justice

There are two kinds of mitzvot. There are the commands of self-restraint that hold us back from damaging the human or natural environment. And there are the positive commands of love, for the world as God's work, and for human beings as God's image. Of the second, the greatest is *tzedaka*: love as justice (sometimes translated as "charity").

The world is not always just, or equitable, or fair. Our task is to make it more so, by helping those in need, sharing some of what we have with others. This act of sharing is more than charity. It is a recognition of the fact that what we have, we have from God, and one of the conditions of God's gifts is that we ourselves give. That way we too become like God, "walking in His ways."

The market creates wealth; that is its virtue. But it does not necessarily distribute it in such a way as to alleviate poverty, granting everyone the means of a dignified life. That is its weakness. There are two possibilities: either abandon the market, or mitigate its negative effects. The first has been tried, and failed. The second can be done in two ways: through the government (taxation, welfare) or through individuals. Governments can do much, but not everything. *Tzedaka* is Judaism's way of saying that each of us has a part to play. Every one of us must give.

Tzedaka means both justice and charity, for we believe that they go hand in hand. Justice is impersonal, charity is personal. We call God *Avinu Malkeinu,* "Our Father, our King." A king dispenses justice; a parent gives a child a gift out of love. That is the meaning of *tzedaka,* an act that combines both justice and love. Giving to others is one of the most beautiful things we can do, and one of the most creative. We create possibilities for other people. We soften some of the rough edges of the world. We help alleviate poverty and pain. We give God the sacrifice He most desires of us: that we honour His image in other people.

Nothing more marks Judaism as a religion of love than its emphasis on *tzedaka*. We do not accept poverty, hunger, homelessness, or disease as God's will. To the contrary, God's will is that we heal these fractures in His world. As God feeds the hungry, so must we. As God heals the sick, so must we. We become good by doing good. We walk in God's ways by acting out of love.

Do Not Harden Your Heart

If there be a poor person among your kinsfolk in any of your towns in the land that the Lord your God is giving you, do not harden your heart or close your hand toward your brother in need. Open your hand generously and freely lend him enough to answer all his needs.... Give to him generously, and do not let your heart begrudge it, for by merit of this the Lord your God will grant you blessing in all your work and all your hands' endeavors. There will never cease to be poor people in the land. And so I command you: open your hand generously to your kinsmen, your poor and needy, who share your land.

Deuteronomy 15:7–11

Treasures of Souls

Our masters taught: It is related of King Monabaz [king of Adiabene in the first century CE who converted to Judaism] that during years of scarcity he spent all his own treasures and the treasures of his fathers on charity. His brothers and other members of his family reproached him: "Your fathers stored away treasures, adding to the treasures of their fathers, and you squander them!" He replied: "My fathers stored away for the world below, while I am storing away for the world above. My fathers stored away in a place where the hand of others can prevail, while I have stored away in a place where the hand of others cannot prevail. My fathers stored away something that produces no fruit, while I have stored away something that does produce fruit. My fathers stored away treasures of money, while I have stored away treasures of souls."

Bava Batra 11a

Admitted to the Divine Presence

R. Dostai ben R. Yannai taught: Consider the difference between the Holy One and a king of flesh and blood. If a man brings a present to the king, it may or may not be accepted. Even if it is accepted, it remains doubtful whether the man will be admitted into the king's presence. Not so with the Holy One. A person who gives even one small coin to a beggar is deemed worthy of being admitted to behold the Divine Presence, as it is written, "I, through charity, shall behold Your face" (Ps. 17:15). R. Elazar used to give a coin to a poor man and only then say his prayers, because, he said, it is written, "I, through charity, shall behold Your face."

Bava Batra 10a

The Strongest Thing

There are ten strong things in the world:
Rock is strong, but iron breaks it.
Iron is strong, but fire melts it.
Fire is strong, but water extinguishes it.
Water is strong, but the clouds carry it.
The clouds are strong, but the wind drives them.
The wind is strong, but man withstands it.
Man is strong, but fear weakens him.
Fear is strong, but wine removes it.

Wine is strong, but sleep overcomes it.
Sleep is strong, but death stands over it.
What is stronger than death?
Acts of charity (*tzedaka*), for it is written, "*Tzedaka* delivers from death" (Prov. 10:2).

Bava Batra 10a

The Ladder of Charity

There are eight degrees of charity, one higher than the other.

The highest degree, exceeded by none, is that of one who assists a poor person by providing him with a gift or a loan or by accepting him into a business partnership or by helping him find employment – in a word, by putting him in a situation where he can dispense with other people's aid. With reference to such aid it is said, "You shall strengthen him; be he a stranger or a Settler, he shall live with you" (Lev. 25:35), which means: Strengthen him in such a manner that his falling into want is prevented.

A step below this is one who gives alms to the needy in such a way that the giver does not know to whom he gives and the recipient does not know from whom he takes. This exemplifies doing a good deed for its own sake. One example was the Hall of Secrecy in the Temple, where the righteous would place their gift clandestinely and where poor people from noble families could come and secretly help themselves to aid. Close to this is putting money in a charity box....

One step lower is where the giver knows to whom he gives, but the poor person does not know from whom he receives. Thus the great sages would go and secretly put money into poor people's doorways....

A step lower is when the poor person knows from whom he is taking, but the giver does not known to whom he is giving. Thus the great sages would tie coins in their scarves, which they would fling over their shoulders, so that the poor could help themselves without suffering shame.

Lower than this is where someone gives the poor person a gift before he asks.

Lower still is one who gives only after the poor person asks.

Lower than this is one who gives less than is fitting, but does so with a friendly countenance.

The lowest level is one who gives ungraciously.

Maimonides, *Mishneh Torah,*
Hilkhot Mattenot Aniyim 10:7–14

We Own What We Are Willing to Share

The fifteenth-century Jewish diplomat and scholar Don Isaac Abrabanel (1437–1508), chancellor to King Ferdinand and Queen Isabella of Castile, was once asked by the king how much he owned. He named a certain sum. "But surely," the king said, "you own much more than that." "You asked me," Abrabanel replied, "how much I owned. The property I have, I do not own. Your majesty may seize it from me tomorrow. At best I am its temporary guardian. The sum I mentioned is what

I have given away in charity. That merit alone, neither you nor any earthly power can take away from me." We own what we are willing to share.

Adapted from Abraham J. Twerski, *Do unto Others*, 26–27

Israel's Two Seas

There is something strange about the geography of the Holy Land. There are two seas in Israel: the Dead Sea and the Sea of Galilee. The latter is full of life: fish, birds, vegetation. The former, as its name suggests, contains no life at all. Yet they are both fed by the same river, the Jordan. The difference is that the Sea of Galilee receives water at one end and gives out water at the other. The Dead Sea receives but does not give. The Jordan ends there. To receive without reciprocating is a kind of death. To live is to give.

Only Human Beings Can Help the Poor

The Kaminker Rebbe once resolved to devote a whole day to reciting Psalms. Towards evening, he was still reciting when a messenger came to tell him that his mentor, the Maggid of Tzidnov, wanted to see him. The Rebbe said he would come as soon as he was finished, but the messenger returned, saying that the Maggid insisted that he come immediately. When he arrived, the Maggid asked him why he had delayed. The Rebbe explained that he had been reciting Psalms. The Maggid told him that he had summoned the Rebbe to collect money for a poor person in need. He continued: "Psalms can be sung by angels, but only human beings can help the poor. Charity is greater than reciting Psalms, because angels cannot perform charity."

Adapted from Reuven Bulka,
Work, Life, Suffering and Death, 185

Prayer

Ribbono shel Olam, Sovereign of the Universe, teach me to share what I have with others, for I have much and they have little. What I have, I have from You. As You have given me what I need, so may I become Your partner by giving others what they need.

6. The Way of *Ḥesed*: Love as Compassion

T*zedaka* is the gift of money or its equivalent. But sometimes that is not what we most need. We can suffer emotional as well as physical poverty. We can be depressed, lonely, close to despair. We may need company or comfort, encouragement or support. These too are human needs, no less real for being untranslatable into the language of politics or economics.

That is what *ḥesed* is about: emotional support, loving-kindness, love as compassion. It is what we mean when we speak of God as one who "heals the brokenhearted and binds up their wounds" (Ps. 147). It includes hospitality to the lonely, visiting the sick, comforting the bereaved, raising the spirits of the depressed, helping people through crises in their lives, and making those at the margins feel part of the community.

It is *tzedaka*'s other side. *Tzedaka* is done with material goods, *ḥesed* with psychological ones: time and care. *Tzedaka* is practical support, *ḥesed* is emotional support. *Tzedaka* is a gift of resources, *ḥesed* a gift of the person. Even those who lack the means to give *tzedaka* can still give *ḥesed*. *Tzedaka* rights wrongs; *ḥesed* humanises fate.

Abraham and Sarah were chosen because of their *ḥesed* to others. Ruth became the ancestress of Israel's kings because of her *ḥesed* to Naomi. At the heart of the Judaic vision is the dream of a society based on *ḥesed*: society with a human face, not one dominated by the competition for wealth or power. *Ḥesed* is the mark of a people joined by covenant. Covenant creates society-as-extended-family; it means seeing strangers as if they were our long-lost brothers or sisters. A community based on *ḥesed* is a place of grace, where everyone feels honoured, everyone is at home.

Loving-Kindness, Not Sacrifice

For it is loving-kindness I yearn for, not sacrifice;
awareness of God rather than burnt offerings.

Hosea 6:6

Walking in God's Ways

R. Ḥama ben R. Ḥanina said: What does [the Torah] mean when it says, "You shall walk after the Lord your God" (Deut. 13:5)? Is it possible for a human being to walk after the Divine Presence? Does it not say, "For the Lord your God is a consuming fire" (Deut. 4:24)?

Rather, the meaning is: You shall walk after the attributes of the Holy One, blessed be He.

Just as He clothes the naked, so shall you clothe the naked. Just as He visits the sick, so you must visit the sick. Just as the Holy One, blessed be, He comforts mourners, so you must comfort mourners. Just as the Holy One, blessed be He, buries the dead, so you must bury the dead.

Sota 14a

Ḥesed Atones

Once, as R. Yoḥanan was walking out of Jerusalem, R. Yehoshua followed him. Seeing the Temple in ruins, he cried, "Woe to us that this place is in ruins, the place where atonement was made for Israel's iniquities." R. Yoḥanan said to him: "My son, do not grieve, for we have another means of atonement which is no less effective. What is it? It is deeds of loving-kindness, about which Scripture says, 'It is loving-kindness I yearn for, not sacrifice' (Hos. 6:6)."

Avot DeRabbi Natan 4

Love Is Never Lost

That which a person gives to another is never lost. It is an extension of his own being. He can see a part of himself in the fellow man to whom he has given. This is the attachment between one person and his fellow to which we give the name "love."

Rabbi Eliyahu Dessler, *Strive for Truth!*, I, 129

A Poor Man's Funeral

Once two Jews died in Brisk on the same day. In the morning a poor shoemaker who had lived out his life in obscurity died, while at about noontime a wealthy, prominent member of the community passed away. According to the halakha, in such a case the one who dies first must be buried first. However, the members of the burial society, who had received a handsome sum from the heirs of the rich man, decided to attend to him first, despite the fact that he had died later, for who was there to plead the cause of the poor man? When Rabbi Hayim [of Brisk] was informed about the incident, he sent a messenger of the court to warn the members of the burial society to desist from their disgraceful behaviour. The members of the burial society, however, refused to heed the directive of R. Hayim and began to make the arrangements for the burial of the rich man. R. Hayim then arose, took his walking stick, trudged over to the house of the deceased, and chased all the attendants outside. R. Hayim prevailed – the poor man was buried before the rich man.

Rabbi Joseph Soloveitchik, *Halakhic Man*, 95

And Maybe Even Higher

Every Friday morning before dawn, the Rebbe of Nemirov would disappear. He could be found in none of the town's synagogues or houses of study. The doors of his house were open but he was not there. Once a

Lithuanian scholar came to Nemirov. Puzzled by the Rebbe's disappearance, he asked his followers, "Where is he?" "Where is the Rebbe?" they replied. "Where else but in heaven? The people of the town need peace, sustenance, health. The Rebbe is a holy man and therefore he is surely in heaven, pleading our cause."

The Lithuanian, amused by their credulity, determined to find out for himself. One Thursday night he hid himself in the Rebbe's house. The next morning before dawn he heard the Rebbe weep and sigh. Then he saw him go to the cupboard, take out a parcel of clothes and begin to put them on. They were the clothes, not of a holy man, but of a peasant. The Rebbe then reached into a drawer, pulled out an axe, and went out into the still dark night. Stealthily, the Lithuanian followed him as he walked through the town and beyond, into the forest. There he began chopping down a tree, hewing it into logs, and splitting it into firewood. These he gathered into a bundle and walked back into the town.

In one of the back streets, he stopped outside a run-down cottage and knocked on the door. An old woman, poor and ill, opened the door. "Who are you?" she said. "I am Vassily," the Rebbe replied. "I have wood to sell, very cheap, next to nothing." "I have no money," replied the woman. "I will give it to you on credit," he said. "How will I be able to pay you?" she said. "I trust you – and do you not trust God? He will find a way of seeing that I am repaid." "But who will light the fire? I am too ill." "I will light the fire," the Rebbe replied, and he did so, reciting under his breath the morning prayers. Then he returned home.

The Lithuanian scholar, seeing this, stayed on in the town and became one of the Rebbe's disciples. After that day, when he heard the people of the town tell visitors that the Rebbe ascended to heaven, he no longer laughed, but added: "And maybe even higher."

Adapted from a short story by Y. L. Peretz

Welcoming the Messiah

At the third Shabbat meal, as the day grew dark and the mood intense, one of the Hasidim turned to the Rebbe with a question he had long wanted to ask but had not had the courage to do so until now. "Rebbe, why does the Messiah not come?" "Why do you ask, my son?" "Because," he replied, "in the past perhaps we were not ready. The world was not ready. The hour was not right. But now, after the Holocaust, and the return of Jews to their land, has the time not come?" "What do you mean?" the Rebbe asked, his face unchanging but his gaze intent.

The Hasid continued: "What I mean is – do we not read in the holy Talmud that at the end of days the Holy One, blessed be He, will bring against the Jewish people a king whose decrees will be as harsh as Haman's – and did that not happen? Was not Hitler just such a king and were his decrees not just as harsh? And did not our holy teacher Moses say that at the end of exile God will gather us in? Did he not say, 'Even if you have been banished to the most distant land under heaven, from there the Lord your God will gather you and bring you back'? And has this too not occurred, now that Jews have returned to Israel from more than a hundred different lands? Why then does the Messiah not come?"

"I will tell you, my son," said the Rebbe. "How *could* the Messiah come? Consider: If he were a Hasid of one sect, the Hasidim of the other sects would not recognise him. If he were a Hasid of any kind, the *mitnagdim*, their opponents, would not recognise him. If he were Orthodox, the Reform Jews would not recognise him. If he were religious, the secular Jews would not recognise him. How then can he come?"

"And now," continued the Rebbe, "I will tell you a great secret." The Rebbe dropped his voice to a whisper. "*It is not we who are waiting for the Messiah. It is the Messiah who is waiting for us*. He has been here all the time. It is we who are not yet ready for him."

Before the Hasid could reply, the Rebbe continued: "And now let me ask you a question. What would you do if the Messiah *did* arrive? Would you not greet him as a long-lost, long-awaited friend? Would you not invite him in as a royal guest and do the utmost to pay him honour and be honoured beyond measure by his presence?" "Of course," replied the Hasid. "Can the Rebbe doubt it?"

"Well," said the Rebbe, "I will tell you what you must do and teach others to do. Regard every person – familiar or a stranger, young or old, learned or unlearned, observant or unobservant – as if he or she might be the Messiah, for the Messiah will surely come in disguise. If only we would do this, we would find that, without our realising it, the Messiah had come."

Jonathan Sacks, *To Heal a Fractured World*, 55–56

Prayer

Ribbono shel Olam, Sovereign of the Universe, help me this year to think more about others and less about myself. Help me to recognise those who need help or company or comfort. Teach me to say the kind word, do the kind deed. Teach me to walk in Your ways.

7. The Way of Faith: Love as Loyalty

Judaism is an unusual, subtle, profoundly humane faith that challenges the conventional wisdom of the ages. Faith is the courage Abraham and Sarah showed when they heard the call of God and left behind all they had known to travel to an unknown destination. Faith led more than a hundred generations of our ancestors to continue that journey, knowing all the risks yet believing there is no greater privilege than to be part of it. Faith is the voice that says, "Though I walk through the valley of the shadow of death I will fear no evil for You are with me."

Faith sustained Jews in the dark days of persecution. It led them never to give up hope that one day they would return to Israel, Jerusalem, and freedom. Jews kept faith alive. Faith kept the Jewish people alive.

Faith is not certainty. It is the courage to live with uncertainty. It is not knowing all the answers. It is often the strength to live with the questions. It is not a sense of invulnerability. It is the knowledge that we are utterly vulnerable, but that it is precisely in our vulnerability that we reach out to God, and through this learn to reach out to others, able to understand their fears and doubts. We learn to share, and in sharing discover the road to freedom. It is only because we are not gods that we are able to discover God.

God is the personal dimension of existence, the "Thou" beneath the "It," the "ought" beyond the "is," the Self that speaks to self in moments of total disclosure. Opening ourselves to the universe we find God reaching out to us. At that moment we make the life-changing discovery that though we seem utterly insignificant, we are utterly significant, a fragment of God's presence in the world. Eternity preceded us, infinity will come after us, yet we know that this day, this moment, this place, this circumstance, is full of the light of infinite radiance, whose proof is the mere fact that we are here to experience it.

Faith is where God and human beings touch across the abyss of infinity. *Emuna* means faithfulness, love-as-loyalty. The closest analogue is marriage: a mutual commitment, entered into in love, binding the partners together in fidelity and trust. God chose us; we chose God; and though our relationship has sometimes been tense and troubled, the bond between us is unbreakable.

Knowing, we are known. Feeling, we are felt. Acting, we are acted upon. Living, we are lived. And if we make ourselves transparent to existence, then our lives too radiate that Divine Presence which, celebrating life, gives life to those whose lives we touch.

Faith is the space we create for God.

Whom Need I Fear?

The Lord is my light and my salvation – whom need I fear? The Lord is the stronghold of my life – whom need I dread? When evildoers close in on me to devour my flesh, it is they, my enemies and foes, who stumble and fall. Should an army besiege me, my heart would not fear. Should war break out against me, I would still be confident.

Psalms 27:1–3

A Jew I Shall Remain

Solomon ibn Verga (Spain-Italy, fifteenth to sixteenth century) was one of the rare Jewish historians of the Middle Ages. In his account of the Spanish Expulsion, he told this story:

I heard from some of the elders who came out of Spain that one of the boats was infested with the plague, and the captain of the boat put the passengers ashore at some uninhabited place. There, most of them died of starvation, while some of them gathered all their strength to set out on foot in search of some settlement.

There was one Jew among them who struggled on afoot together with his wife and two children. The wife grew faint and died, because she was not accustomed to so much difficult walking. The husband carried his children along until both he and they fainted from hunger. When he regained consciousness, he found that his two children had died.

In great grief he rose to his feet and said: "O Lord of all the universe, You are doing a great deal that I might even desert my faith. But know You of a certainty that – even against the will of heaven – a Jew I am and a Jew I shall remain. And neither that which You have brought upon me nor that which You may yet bring upon me will be of any avail."

Thereupon he gathered some earth and some grass, and covered the boys, and went forth in search of a settlement.

Shevet Yehuda, 89–94, cited in Nahum Glatzer, ed., *A Jewish Reader*, 204

Where We Let Him In

Rabbi Menahem Mendel of Kotzk (1787–1859) was one of the most remarkable figures of the Jewish mystical movement known as Hasidism. Angular, unconventional, passionate in his search for truth, he spent his life "wrestling with God and with men."

On one occasion, at the third Shabbat meal, when the atmosphere of the holy day is at its most intense, the Rebbe turned to his disciples and asked, "Where does God live?"

They were stunned by the strangeness of the question. "What does the Rebbe mean, 'Where does God live?' Where does God *not* live? Surely we are taught that there is no place devoid of His presence. He fills the heavens and the earth."

"No," said the Rebbe. "You have not understood. God lives *where we let Him in.*"

God is always here, but we sense Him only when we search. He teaches, but only when we are ready to learn. He speaks, but only when we listen. The question is never "Where is God?" It is always "Where are we?" The problem of faith is not God but humankind. The task of faith is to create an openness in the soul through which the Divine Presence can enter. God lives where we let Him in.

To Light a Fire

The Kotzker said: Some people wear their faith like an overcoat. It only warms them, but does not benefit others at all. But some light a fire, and also warm others.

Rabbi Joseph Schneerson: Two Worlds, One God

Rabbi Joseph Schneerson ran a seminary in Russia. When the communists came to power they ordered all religious seminaries to close. Rabbi Schneerson defied the order and continued teaching religion.

One day a government officer confronted him and ordered him to close his school. The Rebbe refused. The officer pulled out a gun and said, "You will close the school or you will be killed." Rabbi Schneerson showed no emotion and quietly responded, "The school will remain open."

The officer could not help being impressed by the rabbi's calm demeanor and complete lack of fear. "Don't you take me seriously?" he asked. "Aren't you afraid of dying?"

The rabbi responded calmly, "Someone who has only one world and many gods is afraid of dying. Someone who has two worlds and only one God has no fear."

Rabbi Schneerson's yeshiva remained open. In 1940 he transplanted it to the United States. Today it has branches throughout the world. Russian communism is no more.

Adapted from Abraham J. Twerski, *Do Unto Others,* 159

Baron Rothschild: Faith in Freedom

It is told of Baron Nathaniel Rothschild that, after winning his battle of many years to have the disabilities of members of the Jewish faith removed from the House of Lords, he slipped away from the hierarchy of Britain congratulating him on the achievement and was to be found prostrate in prayer in a small synagogue in the Whitechapel ghetto of East London, his lips murmuring, "Would that this freedom shall not mean the diminution of our faith."

Yaacov Herzog, *A People That Dwells Alone*

A Faith of Questions

Isidore Rabi, winner of a Nobel Prize in physics, was once asked why he became a scientist. He replied, "My mother made me a scientist without ever knowing it.

Every other child would come back from school and be asked, 'What did you learn today?' But my mother used to ask a different question. 'Izzy,' she always used to say, 'Did you ask a good question today?' That made the difference. Asking good questions made me a scientist."

Judaism is a religion of questions. The greatest prophets asked questions of God. The book of Job, the most searching of all explorations of human suffering, is a book of questions asked by man, to which God replies with a string of questions of His own. The Seder service on Pesaḥ begins with four questions asked by a child.

When I first went to study at a yeshiva I was struck by the way the teacher's face would light up when we asked a question. *Du fregst a gutte kashe*, "You raise a good objection," was his highest form of praise. Abraham Twerski, an American psychiatrist, tells of how, when he was young, his instructor would relish challenges to his arguments. In his broken English he would say, "You right! You a hundred prozent right! Now I show you where you wrong."

Religious faith, in Judaism, is not naïve or blind. Every question asked in reverence is the start of a journey towards God. When faith suppresses questions, it dies. When it accepts superficial answers, it begins to wither. Faith is not opposed to doubt. What it is opposed to is the shallow certainty that what we understand is all there is.

Jonathan Sacks, *Celebrating Life*, 79–81

Faith After the Holocaust

Rabbi Yekutiel Halberstam, the Klausenberger Rebbe, lived through the Warsaw Ghetto, the work camps, the death march to Dachau, and then Auschwitz itself. He survived, but his wife and eleven children did not. In Auschwitz, he vowed that if he survived he would dedicate himself to life. He resolved to build a hospital that would honour the image of God in every human being. It took him fifteen years to raise the money, but eventually he built the Laniado Hospital in Netanya, Israel, dedicated to treating everyone alike, Jew and Arab, Israeli and Palestinian. This is what he taught his followers after the Holocaust:

The biggest miracle of all is the one that we, the survivors of the Holocaust, after all that we witnessed and lived through, still believe and have faith in the Almighty God, may His name be blessed. This, my friends, is the miracle of miracles, the greatest miracle ever to have taken place.

Yaffa Eliach, *Hassidic Tales of the Holocaust,* 228

Prayer

Ribbono shel Olam, Sovereign of the Universe, teach me to have faith in You as You have faith in me. Open my ears to Your voice, my eyes to Your wonders, my heart to Your love.

8. The Way of Israel: The Jewish Land

No religion in history has been as closely tied to a land as has Judaism. That connection goes back four thousand years, from the first words of God to Abraham: "Leave your country, your birthplace, and your father's house and go to the land that I will show you." No sooner had he arrived than God said: "To your offspring I will give this land." Seven times God promised the land to Abraham, and promised it again to Isaac and Jacob.

The word *teshuva,* often translated as "repentance," literally means "homecoming" in a double sense: spiritually to God, and physically to the Land of Israel. For Israel is the Jewish people's place of destiny: a tiny land for a tiny people, yet one whose role in religious history is vast. It is the land to which Moses and the Israelites travelled across the desert, the land from which they were exiled twice, the land to which our ancestors journeyed whenever they could and which they never voluntarily left, never relinquished. Jewish history is the story of the longing for a land.

The Holy Land remains the place where Jews were summoned to create a society of justice and compassion under the sovereignty of God. And though it was subsequently held holy by Christianity and Islam, it was so only in a derivative sense – because it was the land promised to Abraham, from whom first Christians, then Muslims, claimed to be descended. The centres of these other faiths were elsewhere: for Western Christians, Rome, for Eastern Christians, Constantinople, for Muslims, Mecca and Medina. There are fifty-six Islamic states today, eighty-two Christian ones, but only one Jewish state. It is the only place on earth where Jews are a majority, where they enjoy self-rule, where they are able to build a society and shape a culture as Jews.

The Balfour Declaration in 1917, subsequently ratified by the League of Nations, long before the Holocaust, was an attempt to rectify the single most sustained crime against humanity: the denial of a nation's right to its land and the subsequent persecution of Jews in country after country, century after century, in a history of suffering that has no parallel.

The Jews who returned were not strangers, outsiders, an imperial presence, a colonial force. They were the land's original inhabitants: the only people in four thousand years who created an independent nation there. All other occupiers of the land – from the Assyrians and Babylonians to the Ottomans and British – were imperial powers, who ruled the land as a district of their vast realms. The Egyptians did not offer the Palestinians a state when they ruled Gaza between

1948 and 1967; neither did the Jordanians when they ruled the West Bank during those years. The only nation to have offered Palestinians a state is the State of Israel. We pray for its peace.

Moses' Prophecy of Return

If you should be expelled to the furthest of horizons, even from there the Lord your God will gather you, from there He will take you back.

Deuteronomy 30:4

The Exiles' Lament: By the Rivers of Babylon

By the rivers of Babylon, there we sat and wept
as we remembered Zion....
How can we sing the Lord's song
on foreign soil?
If I forget you, O Jerusalem,
may my right hand forget its skill.
May my tongue cling to the roof of my mouth
if I do not remember you,
if I do not set Jerusalem
above my highest joy.

Psalms 137

Amos' Vision

"I will bring back the exiled of My nation, Israel.
They will build ruined cities and settle.
They will plant vineyards and drink their wine.
They will grow gardens and eat their fruit.
I will plant them on their land,

and never again will they be uprooted
from the land which I gave to them,"
says the Lord, your God.

Amos 9:14–15

Napoleon's Call

In 1798 Napoleon began his campaign in the Middle East, landing first in Egypt, then in Palestine. With a strong sense of history, he realised that this could herald the return of Jews to the land from which they had been exiled for so long. He sent this message to the Jews:

Thousands of years of conquest and tyranny have deprived you of your ancestral lands. Yet for all the time you have somehow continued to exist as a nation. Long ago when the prophets Joel and Isaiah saw the approaching destruction of their fatherland they also foretold the day it would be restored. Now at last that day has dawned. Arise with gladness, ye heirs of Palestine. A great nation [France] calls on you to take on what has been conquered and to remain as masters there, defending it against all comers. Hasten! Now is the moment which may not return for generations to claim back the rights you have been deprived of for thousands of years, to live again as a nation among nations.

Premier Floreal (April 20) 1799; quoted by F. Kobler, "Napoleon and the Restoration of the Jews to Palestine," in *The New Judaea*, September 1940, 190

Chateaubriand

Soon after Napoleon's campaign, the French historian Chateaubriand visited Jerusalem. There he found a tiny Jewish community whose persistence filled him with awe. Speaking of the Jewish settlement, he wrote:

It has seen Jerusalem destroyed seventeen times, yet there exists nothing in the world which can discourage it or prevent it from raising its eyes to Zion. He who beholds the Jews dispersed over the face of the earth, in keeping with the Word of God, lingers and marvels. But he will be struck with amazement, as at a miracle, who finds them still in Jerusalem and perceives even, who in law and justice are the masters of Judea, to exist as slaves and strangers in their own land; how despite all abuses they await the king who is to deliver them.... If there is anything among the nations of the world marked with the stamp of the miraculous, this, in our opinion, is that miracle.

R. Mahler, *A History of Modern Jewry 1780–1815*, 621

Emir Faisal

Not all Arab leaders were opposed to Zionism. Some recognised the historic connection between Jews and the Land of Israel. They knew that a Jewish presence could bring prosperity to the whole area. This letter was written by King Faisal to the American Jewish judge Felix Frankfurter on March 3, 1919:

We feel that the Arabs and Jews are cousins in race, having suffered similar oppressions at the hands of powers stronger than themselves, and by a happy coincidence have been able to take the first step towards the attainment of their national ideals together.

We Arabs, especially the educated among us, look with the deepest sympathy on the Zionist movement.... We will do our best, in so far as we are concerned, to help them through: we will wish the Jews a most hearty welcome home....

We are working together for a reformed and revived Near East, and our two movements complete one another. The Jewish movement is national and not imperialist. Our movement is national and not imperialist, and there is room in Syria [the name given at that time to the whole area that is now Syria, Lebanon, Jordan, and Israel] for us both. Indeed I think that neither can be a real success without the other....

I look forward, and my people with me look forward, to a future in which we will help you and you will help us, so that the countries in which we are mutually interested may once again take their places in the community of civilised peoples of the world.

In Walter Laqueur and Barry Rubin, eds., *The Israel-Arab Reader,* 19–20

Winston Churchill: For the Good of All the World

I believe that the establishment of a Jewish National Home in Palestine will be a blessing to the whole world, a blessing to the Jewish race scattered all over the world, and a blessing to Great Britain.... The hope of your race for so many centuries will be gradually realised here, not only for your own good, but for the good of all the world.

Speech at Mount Scopus, March 29, 1921,
in Martin Gilbert, *Churchill and the Jews*, 56–57

1948: Israel's Declaration of Independence

From the outset, Israel sought peace with its neighbours. It accepted the various plans for partition in the 1920s and 1930s; it accepted the partition proposal of the United Nations in 1947. Its neighbours rejected all proposals. The offer of peace was renewed soon after the Six-Day War. The response of the Arab League, meeting in Khartoum in September 1967, was the famous "Three Nos": no to peace, no to negotiations, no to the recognition of the State of Israel. The call to peace was a central strand of Israel's Declaration of Independence in May 1948:

Eretz Yisrael [the Land of Israel] was the birthplace of the Jewish people. Here their spiritual, religious, and political identity was shaped. Here they first attained to statehood, created cultural values of national and universal significance, and gave to the world the eternal Book of Books.

After being forcibly exiled from their land, the people kept faith with it throughout their dispersion and never ceased to pray and hope for their return to it and for the restoration in it of their political freedom....

We appeal – in the very midst of the onslaught launched against us now for months – to the Arab inhabitants of the State of Israel to preserve peace and participate in the upbuilding of the State on the basis of full and equal citizenship and due representation in all its provisional and permanent institutions.

We extend our hand to all neighbouring states and their peoples in an offer of peace and good neighbourliness, and appeal to them to establish bonds of cooperation and mutual help with the sovereign Jewish people settled in its own land. The State of Israel is prepared to do its share in a common effort for the advancement of the entire Middle East.... Placing our trust in the "Rock of Israel," we affix our signatures to this proclamation at this session of the provisional Council of State, on the soil of the homeland, in the city of Tel Aviv, on this Sabbath eve, the fifth day of Iyar 5708 (May 14, 1948).

Yitzhak Rabin: Enough of Blood and Tears

In September 1993, then prime minister of Israel Yitzhak Rabin shook hands with Yasser Arafat on the White House lawn, marking the start of what was hoped to be a peace process. It was not to be. Within a year Israel suffered its first suicide bombing. In 1995 Rabin himself was assassinated. The speech he made that day is one of the greatest speeches of the twentieth century.

We have come from Jerusalem, the ancient and eternal capital of the Jewish people. We have come from an anguished and grieving land. We have come from a people, a home, a family, that has not known a single year – not a single month – in which mothers have not wept for their sons. We have come to try and put an end to the hostilities, so that our children and our children's children will no longer have to experience the painful cost of war, violence, and terror. We have come to secure their lives, and to ease the sorrow and the painful memories of the past – to hope and pray for peace.

Let me say to you, the Palestinians: We are destined to live together, on the same soil in the same land. We, the soldiers who have returned from battle stained with blood, we who have seen our relatives and friends killed before our eyes, we who have attended their funerals and cannot look into the eyes of their parents, we who have come from a land where parents bury their children, we who have fought against you, the Palestinians – we say to you today in a loud and clear voice: Enough of blood and tears. Enough.

We have no desire for revenge. We harbour no hatred towards you. We, like you, are people who want to build a home, to plant a tree, to love, to live side by side with you – in dignity, in empathy, as human beings, as free men. We are today giving peace a chance and again saying to you: Let us pray that a day will come when we will say, enough, farewell to arms.

We wish to turn over a new chapter in the sad book of our lives together – a chapter of mutual recognition, of good neighbourliness, of mutual respect, of understanding. We hope to embark on a new era in the history of the Middle East. Today, here in Washington, at the White House, we will begin a new reckoning in relations between peoples, between parents tired of war, between children who will not know war.

President of the United States, ladies and gentlemen, our inner strength, our higher moral values, have been derived for thousands of years from the Book of Books, in one of which, Ecclesiastes, we read: "To every thing there is a season, and a time to every purpose under heaven: A time to be born, and a time to die; A time to kill, and a time to heal; A time to weep, and a time to laugh; A time to love, and a time to hate; A time for war, and a time for peace." Ladies and gentlemen, the time for peace has come.

Prayer

Ribbono shel Olam, Sovereign of the Universe, send peace to the land and people of Israel. Let the bloodshed end. Let the hate end. Let Israel be what for four thousand years it was meant to be: the place where the people of Your covenant could build a society to honour the dignity of man under the sovereignty of God.

9. The Way of *Kiddush Hashem*: The Jewish Task

The way of Judaism is particular; the concern of Judaism is universal. Abraham was promised that "through you all the families of the earth will be blessed." Isaiah said that we are called on to be God's "witnesses." Our message is not for ourselves alone.

How so? We do not seek to convert others. We believe that the righteous of all nations have a share in the World to Come. But we do seek to be living examples, reflections of God's light, an inspiration to others to find their own way to God. That, we believe, is the only way of honouring the fact, after Babel, of a world of many cultures and civilisations. God is One; we are many; and we must learn to live together in peace. That is why we do not seek to impose our faith on others. Truth is communicated by influence, not power, by example, not by force or fear.

Others have understood this about us, and the quotations in this chapter are testimony to this fact. Winston Churchill said that the West owes to the Jews "a system of ethics which, even it were entirely separated from the supernatural, would be incomparably the most precious possession of mankind, worth in fact the fruits of all other learning and wisdom put together."

At a time when we have witnessed the resurgence of antisemitism, the world's oldest hatred, it is important to know that, yes, we have enemies but we also have friends. We have critics, but there are those who, without seeking to become Jewish, have drawn inspiration from Jewish life. We owe it to them, not just to ourselves, to be faithful to our task: to be God's ambassadors on earth.

Rousseau: An Astonishing Phenomenon

Jean-Jacques Rousseau (1712–1778) was one of the most influential political thinkers in modern times: his work The Social Contract helped inspire the French Revolution. After his death, the following note was discovered among his unpublished papers.

But an astonishing and truly unique spectacle is to see an expatriated people, who have had neither place nor land for nearly two thousand years, a people mingled with foreigners, no longer perhaps having a single descendant of the early races, a scattered people, dispersed over the world, enslaved, persecuted, scorned by all nations, nonetheless preserving its characteristics, its laws, its customs, its patriotic love of the early social union, when all ties with it seem broken. The Jews provide us with an astonishing spectacle: the laws of Numa, Lycurgus, Solon are dead; the very much older laws of Moses are still alive. Athens, Sparta, Rome have perished and no longer have children left on earth; Zion, destroyed, has not lost its children.

They mingle with all the nations and never merge with them; they no longer have leaders, and are still a nation; they no longer have a homeland, and are always citizens of it.... Any man whosoever he is, must acknowledge this as a unique marvel, the causes of which, divine or human, certainly deserve the study and admiration of the sages, in preference to all that Greece and Rome offer of what is admirable in the way of political institutions and human settlements.

The manuscript is to be found in the public library at Neuchâtel
(*Cahiers de brouillons, notes et extraits*, no. 7843)

President John Adams: Jews and Civilisation

John Adams (1735–1826) was America's first vice president (1789–1797) and second president (1797–1801).

I will insist that the Hebrews have done more to civilize men than any other nation. If I were an atheist, and believed in blind eternal fate, I should still believe that fate had ordained the Jews to be the most essential instrument for civilizing the nations. If I were an atheist of the other sect, who believe or pretend to believe that all is ordered by chance, I should believe that chance had ordered the Jews to preserve and propagate to all mankind the doctrine of a supreme, intelligent, wise, almighty sovereign of the universe, which I believe to be the great essential principle of all morality, and consequently of all civilization.

President John Adams to F. A. Vanderkemp, February 16, 1809, in *The Works of John Adams*, ed. C. F. Adams, vol. 9, 609–10

Leo Tolstoy: As Everlasting as Eternity Itself

Leo Tolstoy (1828–1910), author of War and Peace and Anna Karenina, was perhaps the greatest novelist of all time. In 1877 he had an intense religious experience and thereafter devoted most of his life to religion and a new vision of society which influenced some of the early Zionists as well as Gandhi and Martin Luther King.

The Jew is that sacred being who has brought down from heaven the everlasting fire and has illuminated with it the entire world. He is the religious source, spring, and fountain out of which all the rest of the peoples have drawn their beliefs and their religions.... The Jew is the emblem of eternity. He whom neither slaughter nor torture of thousands of years could destroy, he whom neither fire nor sword nor inquisition was able to wipe off the face of the earth, he who was the first to produce the oracles of God, he who has been for so long the guardian of prophecy, and who has transmitted it to the rest of the world – such a nation cannot be destroyed. The Jew is as everlasting as eternity itself.

Letter found in the archives of the Bulgarian statesman F. Gabai. Text in Allan Gould, *What Did They Think of the Jews,* 180–81

Mark Twain: All Things Are Mortal but the Jew

Mark Twain was the pen name of American novelist Samuel Langhorne Clemens (1835–1910). The following famous passage is taken from a magazine article he wrote in 1899 in answer to a request to clarify his views about the Jews.

If the statistics are right, the Jews constitute but one percent of the human race. It suggests a nebulous dim puff of star dust lost in the blaze of the Milky Way.

Properly the Jew ought hardly to be heard of; but he is heard of, has always been heard of. He is as prominent on the planet as any other people, and his commercial importance is extravagantly out of proportion to the smallness of his bulk.

His contributions to the world's list of great names in literature, science, art, music, finance, medicine, and abstruse learning are also away out of proportion to the weakness of his numbers.

He has made a marvellous fight in this world, in all the ages; and has done it with his hands tied behind him. He could be vain of himself, and be excused for it. The Egyptian, the Babylonian, and the Persian rose, filled the planet with sound and splendor, then faded to dream-stuff and passed away; the Greek and the Roman followed, and made a vast noise, and they are gone; other peoples have sprung up and held their torch high for a time, but it burned out, and they sit in twilight now, or have vanished. The Jew saw them all, beat them all, and is now what he always was, exhibiting no decadence, no infirmities of age, no weakening of his parts, no slowing of his energies, no dulling of his alert and aggressive mind.

All things are mortal but the Jew; all other forces pass, but he remains. What is the secret of his immortality?

Mark Twain, "Concerning the Jews,"
Harper's Magazine, June 1899

Nicolai Berdyaev: The Refutation of Materialism

Nicolai Berdyaev (1874–1948) was a Marxist who held the chair in philosophy at the University of Moscow. In later life he rejected Marxism and became increasingly devoted to religion. In The Meaning of History *he tells of how he came to realise that the history of the Jews refuted the Marxist belief that the destiny of civilisations was ruled by material forces alone.*

I remember how the materialist interpretation of history, when I attempted in my youth to verify it by applying it to the destinies of peoples, broke down in the case of the Jews, where destiny seemed absolutely inexplicable from the materialistic standpoint.... Its survival is a mysterious and wonderful phenomenon demonstrating that the life of this people is governed by a special predetermination, transcending the processes of adaptation expounded by the materialistic interpretation of history. The survival of the Jews, their resistance to destruction, their endurance under absolutely peculiar conditions and the fateful role played by them in history: all these point to the particular and mysterious foundations of their destiny.

Nicolai Berdyaev, *The Meaning of History*, 1936, 86–87

Winston Churchill

Some people like the Jews, and some do not. But no thoughtful man can deny the fact that they are beyond question the most formidable and the most remarkable race which has ever appeared in the world.

Martin Gilbert, *Churchill and the Jews*, 308

Paul Johnson

Paul Johnson (1928–2023) was a Catholic historian, former editor of the New Statesman, and author of A History of the Jews, from which these passages are taken.

No people has ever insisted more firmly than the Jews that history has a purpose and humanity a destiny. At a very early stage in their collective existence they believed they had detected a Divine scheme for the human race, of which their own society was to be a pilot. They worked out their role in immense detail. They clung to it with heroic persistence in the face of savage suffering. Many of them believe it still. Others transmuted it into Promethean endeavours to raise our condition by purely human means. The Jewish vision became the prototype for many similar grand designs for humanity, both Divine and man-made. The Jews, therefore, stand right at the centre of the perennial attempt to give human life the dignity of a purpose.

All the great conceptual discoveries of the intellect seem obvious and inescapable once they have been revealed, but it requires a special genius to formulate them for the first time. The Jews had this gift. To them we owe the idea of equality before the law, both Divine and human; of the sanctity of life and the dignity of the human person; of the individual conscience and so of personal redemption; of the collective conscience and so of social responsibility; of peace as an abstract ideal and love as the foundation of justice, and many other items which constitute the basic moral furniture of the human mind. Without the Jews it might have been a much emptier place.

Paul Johnson, *A History of the Jews*, 2, 585

William Rees-Mogg

Lord Rees-Mogg (1928–2012) was an author, journalist, and former editor of The Times.

One of the gifts of Jewish culture to Christianity is that it has taught Christians to think like Jews, and any modern man who has not learned to think as though he were a Jew can hardly be said to have learned to think at all.

William Rees-Mogg, *The Reigning Error*, 11

A. L. Rowse

A. L. Rowse (1903–1997), Fellow of All Souls, was a historian, poet, Shakespeare scholar, and author of some one hundred books. The following remark is the penultimate sentence of a book published shortly before he died.

If there is any honour in all the world that I should like, it would be to be an honorary Jewish citizen.

A. L. Rowse, *Historians I Have Known*, 1995

Thomas Cahill: Shapers of the West

Cahill, a Catholic historian, studied Judaism for two years in preparation for his book The Gifts of the Jews, from which the following passages are taken.

> The Jews started it all – and by "it" I mean so many of the things we care about, the underlying values that make all of us, Jew and gentile, believer and atheist, tick. Without the Jews, we would see the world through different eyes, hear with different ears, even feel with different feelings....
>
> For better or worse, the role of the West in humanity's history is singular. Because of this, the role of the Jews, the inventors of Western culture, is also singular: there is simply no one else remotely like them; theirs is a unique vocation. Indeed, as we shall see, the very idea of *vocation,* of a personal destiny, is a Jewish idea. The Jews gave us the Outside and the Inside – our outlook and our inner life. We can hardly get up in the morning or cross the street without being Jewish. We dream Jewish dreams and hope Jewish hopes. Most of our best words, in fact – *new, adventure, surprise; unique, individual, person, vocation; time, history, future; freedom, progress, spirit; faith, hope, justice* – are the gifts of the Jews.
>
> Thomas Cahill, *The Gifts of the Jews,* 3, 240–41

Andrew Marr: Stories for the Rest of Us

Andrew Marr (1959–) is a journalist, political philosopher, and broadcaster. The following is taken from an article he wrote for The Observer.

The Jews have always had stories for the rest of us. They have had their Bible, one of the great imaginative works of the human spirit. They have been victim of the worst modernity can do, a mirror for Western madness. Above all they have had the story of their cultural and genetic survival from the Roman Empire to the 2000s, weaving and thriving amid uncomprehending, hostile European tribes.

This story, their post-Bible, their epic of bodies, not words, involved an intense competitive hardening of generations which threw up, in the end, a blaze of individual geniuses in Europe and America. Outside painting, Morris dancing and rap music, it's hard to think of many areas of Western endeavour where Jews haven't been disproportionately successful. For non-Jews, who don't believe in a people being chosen by God, the lesson is that generations of people living on their wits and hard work, outside the more comfortable mainstream certainties, will seed Einsteins and Wittgensteins, Trotskys and Sieffs. Culture matters.... The Jews really have been different; they have enriched the world and challenged it.

Andrew Marr, *The Observer,* Sunday, May 14, 2000

Prayer

Ribbono shel Olam, Sovereign of the Universe, help me to act so as to bring honour to Your name.

10. The Way of Responsibility: The Jewish Future

For every Jew today there are 183 Christians and one hundred Muslims. More than three thousand years later, the words of Moses remain true (Deut. 7:7): "The Lord did not set His affection on you and choose you because you were more numerous than other peoples, for you were the fewest of peoples." We were then. We are now.

Why did God choose this tiny people for so great a task, to be His witnesses in the world, the people who fought against the idols of the age in every age, the carriers of His message to humanity? Why are we so few? Why this dissonance between the greatness of the task and the smallness of the people charged with carrying it out?

There is a strange passage in the Torah: "When you take a census of the Israelites to count them, each one must pay the Lord a ransom for his life at the time he is counted. Then no mishap (*negef*) will come on them when you number them" (Ex. 30:12). The implication is unmistakable. *It is dangerous to count Jews.* Centuries later, King David ignored the warning and disaster struck the nation. Why is it dangerous to count Jews?

Nations take censuses on the assumption that there is strength in numbers. The larger the people, the stronger it is. That is why it is dangerous to count Jews. If Jews ever believed that their strength lay in numbers, we would give way, God forbid, to despair. In Israel they were always a minor power surrounded by great empires. In the Diaspora, everywhere they were a minority.

Where then did Jewish strength lie if not in numbers? The Torah gives an answer of surpassing beauty. God tells Moses: Do not count Jews. *Ask them to give, and then count the contributions.* In terms of numbers we are small. But in terms of our contributions, we are vast. In almost every age, Jews have given something special to the world: the Torah, the literature of the prophets, the poetry of the Psalms, the rabbinic wisdom of the Mishna, Midrash, and Talmud, the vast medieval library of commentaries and codes, philosophy and mysticism. Then, as the doors of Western society opened, Jews made their mark in one field after another: business, industry, the arts and sciences, cinema, the media, medicine, law, and almost every field of academic life. They revolutionised thought in physics, economics, sociology, anthropology, and psychology. Jews have won Nobel Prizes out of all proportion to our numbers.

The simplest explanation is that *to be a Jew is to be asked to give,* to contribute, to make a difference, to help in the monumental task that has engaged Jews since the dawn of our history, to make the world a home for the Divine Presence, a place of justice, compassion, human dignity, and the sanctity of life. Though our ancestors cherished their relationship with God, they never saw it as a privilege. They knew it was a responsibility. God asked great things of the Jewish people, and in so doing, made them great.

When it comes to making a contribution, numbers do not count. What matters is commitment, passion, dedication to a cause. Precisely because we are so small as a people, every one of us counts. We each make a difference to the fate of Judaism and the Jewish people. Zechariah said it best: "Not by might nor by power but by My spirit, says the Almighty Lord."

Physical strength needs numbers. The larger the nation, the more powerful it is. But when it comes to spiritual strength, you need not numbers but a sense of responsibility. You need a people, each of whom knows that he or she must contribute something to the Jewish and to the human story. The Jewish question is not "What can the world give me?" It is "What can I give to the world?" Judaism is God's call to responsibility.

I Am Here

Then I heard the voice of the Lord saying, "Whom shall I send? And who will go for us?" And I said, "I am here. Send me!"

Isaiah 6:8

Do Not Be a Bystander

Do not stand by while your neighbor's life is in danger; I am the Lord.

Leviticus 19:16

Mordecai and Esther: Taking Responsibility

They told Mordecai what Esther had said. Mordecai sent back his reply to Esther: "Do not imagine that you can escape to the king's palace from the fate of all the Jews. For if you keep your silence at this time, relief and salvation will come forth for the Jews from some other place, but you and your father's house will be lost forever. And who can say; could it not be for just such a time as this that you came into royalty?"

Esther 4:12–14

Sharing a Fate

A man in a boat began to bore a hole under his seat. His fellow passengers protested. "What concern is it of yours?" he responded. "I am making a hole under my seat, not yours." They replied, "That is so, but when the water enters and the boat sinks, we too will drown."

Leviticus Rabba 4:6

The Great Principle

All Israel are sureties for one another.

Sifra, Beḥukkotai 2:7

Hillel's Wisdom

Hillel used to say: If I am not for myself, who will be for me? And if I am only for myself, what am I? And if not now, when?

Ethics of the Fathers 1:14

Our Next Act Can Change the World

Throughout the year, everyone should see himself and the world as if evenly poised between innocence and guilt. If he commits a sin he tilts the balance of his fate and that of the world to guilt, causing destruction. If he performs a good deed he shifts the balance of his fate and that of the world to innocence, bringing salvation and deliverance to others. That is the meaning of [the biblical phrase] "The righteous person is the foundation of the world" (Prov. 10:25), namely that by an act of righteousness we influence the fate of, and save, the world.

Maimonides, *Mishneh Torah, Hilkhot Teshuva* 3:4

Martin Niemoeller: No One Left to Speak Up

In Germany they came first for the communists, and I didn't speak up because I wasn't a communist. Then they came for the Jews, and I didn't speak up because I wasn't a Jew. Then they came for the trade unionists, and I didn't speak up because I wasn't a trade unionist. Then they came for the Catholics, and I didn't speak up because I was a Protestant. Then they came for me, and by that time no one was left to speak up.

The Starfish

An old man was walking on the beach at dawn when he noticed a young man picking up starfish stranded by the retreating tide, and throwing them back into the sea one by one. He went up to him and asked him why he was doing this. The young man replied that the starfish would die if left exposed to the morning sun. "But the beach goes on for miles, and there are thousands of starfish. You will not be able to save them all. How can your effort make a difference?" The young man looked at the starfish in his hand and then threw it to safety in the waves. "To *this one,"* he said, "it makes a difference."

Loren Eiseley, *The Star Thrower*

The Righteous Do Not Complain

The pure and righteous do not complain about wickedness: they increase righteousness. They do not complain about heresy: they increase faith. They do not complain about ignorance: they increase wisdom.

Rabbi Avraham Kook, *Arpilei Tohar* 2:99

To Save the Oppressed

Once Rabbi Hayim of Brisk was asked what the function of a rabbi is. Rabbi Hayim replied: "To redress the grievances of those who are abandoned and alone, to protect the dignity of the poor, and to save the oppressed from the hand of his oppressor."

Rabbi Joseph Soloveitchik, *Halakhic Man, 91*

Rabbi Tarfon: It Is Not for You to Complete the Task

Rabbi Tarfon said: The day is short, the task is great, the labourers are lazy, the reward is much, and the Master insistent. He used to say: It is not for you to complete the task, but neither are you free to stand aside from it.

Ethics of the Fathers 2:20–21

A Blessing to Others

To be a Jew is to be alert to the poverty, the suffering, the loneliness of others. Karl Marx called religion "the opium of the people." No religion is less so than Judaism. Opium desensitises us to pain. Judaism sensitises us to it.

No Jew who has lived Judaism can be without a social conscience. To be a Jew is to accept responsibility. The world will not get better of its own accord. Nor will we make it a more human place by leaving it to others – politicians, columnists, protestors, campaigners – making them our agents to bring redemption on our behalf. Life is God's question; our choices are the answer.

To be a Jew is to be a blessing to others. That is what God told Abraham in the first words He spoke to him, words that four thousand years ago set Jewish history into motion. "Through you," He said, "all the families on earth will be blessed." To be a Jew is not to ask for a blessing. It is to be a blessing.

Judaism is about creating spiritual energy, the energy that, if used for the benefit of others, changes lives and begins to change the world. Jewish life is not the search for personal salvation. It is a restless desire to change the world into a place in which God can feel at home. There are a thousand ways in which we help to do this, and each is precious, one not more so than another.

When we give, when we say, "If this is wrong, let me be among the first to help put it right," we create moments of imperishable moral beauty. We know how small we are, and how inadequate to the tasks God has set us. Even the greatest Jew of all time, Moses, began his conversation with God with the words "Who am I?" But it is not we who start by being equal to the challenge; it is the challenge that makes us equal to it. We are as big as our ideals. The higher they are, the taller we stand.

Jonathan Sacks, *From Renewal to Responsibility*

Prayer

Ribbono shel Olam, Sovereign of the Universe, help me act so that in the coming year I am able to say: I heard, I responded, I gave, I grew. Write us, so that we may write others, in the Book of Life.

Epilogue: Why I Am a Jew

I am proud to be a Jew. Pride is not arrogance. Arrogance is the belief that you are better than others. Pride is simply knowing that each of us is different and being at ease with that fact, never "desiring this man's gift and that man's scope." Arrogance diminishes others, and therefore diminishes us. Pride values others, because we have learned to value ourselves.

I learned this lesson from an old Israeli boatman in Eilat. We had gone there, my wife and I, to find the sun after a cold northern winter. Eilat is set in the desert among brown and barren hills. One morning we decided to go out in one of the glass-bottomed boats, through which you can see the multicolored fish that swim in Eilat's waters. We were the only passengers on that trip.

The captain overheard us talking, and rushed over to us. *Atem miAnglia?* "Are you from England?" Yes, we said. Why did he want to know? Ah, he said, I have just come back from a holiday there. What did he think of England? "Wonderful! The grass – so green! The buildings – so old! The people – so polite!" And then a vast smile filled his face, and he spread his arms and looked around him at the barren desert hills and said, with an air of infinite delight, *Aval zeh shelanu,* "But this is ours."

Then I knew what it is to be a Jew. There are other cultures, other civilisations, other peoples, other faiths. Each has contributed something unique to the total experience of mankind. Jews didn't write Shakespeare's sonnets or Beethoven's quartets. We did not give the world the serene beauty of a Japanese garden or the architecture of ancient Greece. I love these things and admire the traditions that brought them forth. *Aval zeh shelanu,* but this is ours. This is our faith, our people, our heritage. By loving them I learn to love humanity in its diversity. At peace with myself, I find peace with the world.

I am a Jew not because of antisemitism or to avoid giving Hitler a posthumous victory. What happens to me does not define who I am: ours is a people of faith, not fate. Nor is it because I think that Jews are better than others, more intelligent, virtuous, law-abiding, creative, generous, or successful. The difference lies not in Jews but Judaism, not in what we are but in what we are called on to be.

I am a Jew because, being a child of my people, I have heard the call to add my chapter to its unfinished story. I am a stage on its journey, a connecting link between the generations. The dreams and hopes of my ancestors live on in me, and I am the guardian of their trust, now and for the future.

I am a Jew because our ancestors were the first to see that the world is driven by a moral purpose, that reality is not a ceaseless war of the elements, to be worshipped as gods, nor history a battle in which might is right and power is to be appeased. The Judaic tradition shaped the moral civilisation of the West, teaching for the first time that human life is sacred, that the individual may never be sacrificed for the mass, and that rich and poor, great and small, are all equal before God.

I am a Jew because I am the heir of those who stood at the foot of Mount Sinai and pledged themselves to live by these truths, becoming a kingdom of priests and a holy nation. I am the descendant of countless generations of ancestors who, though sorely tested and bitterly tried, remained faithful to that covenant when they might so easily have defected.

I am a Jew because of Shabbat, the world's greatest religious institution, a time in which there is no manipulation of nature or our fellow human beings, in which we come together in freedom and equality to create, every week, an anticipation of the Messianic Age.

I am a Jew because our nation, though at times it suffered the deepest poverty, never gave up on its commitment to helping the poor, or rescuing Jews from other lands, or fighting for justice for the oppressed, and did so without self-congratulation, because it was a mitzva, because a Jew could do no less.

I am a Jew because I cherish the Torah, knowing that God is to be found not in natural forces but in moral meanings, in words, texts, teachings and commands, and because Jews, though they lacked all else, never ceased to value education as a sacred task, endowing the individual with dignity and depth.

I am a Jew because of our people's passionate faith in freedom, holding that each of us is a moral agent, and that in this lies our unique dignity as human beings; and because Judaism never left its ideals at the level of lofty aspirations, but instead translated them into deeds which we call mitzvot, and a way, which we call the halakha, and thus brought heaven down to earth.

I am proud, simply, to be a Jew.

I am proud to be part of a people who, though scarred and traumatised, never lost their humour or their faith, their ability to laugh at present troubles and still believe in ultimate redemption; who saw human history as a journey, and never stopped travelling and searching.

I am proud to be part of an age in which my people, ravaged by the worst crime ever to be committed against a people, responded by reviving a land, recovering their sovereignty, rescuing threatened Jews throughout the world, rebuilding Jerusalem, and proving themselves to be as courageous in the pursuit of peace as in defending themselves in war.

I am proud that our ancestors refused to be satisfied with premature consolations, and in answer to the question, "Has the Messiah come?" always answered, "Not yet."

I am proud to belong to the people Israel, whose name means "one who wrestles with God and with man and prevails." For though we have loved humanity, we have never stopped wrestling with it, challenging the idols of every age. And though we have loved God with an everlasting love, we have never stopped wrestling with Him nor He with us.

And though I admire other civilisations and faiths, and believe each has brought something special into the world, still this is my people, my heritage, my God. In our uniqueness lies our universality. Through being what we alone are, we give to humanity what only we can give.

This is our story, our gift to the next generation. I received it from my parents and they from theirs across great expanses of space and time. There is nothing quite like it. It changed and still challenges the moral imagination of mankind. I want to say to the next generation: Take it, cherish it, learn to understand and to love it. Carry it and it will carry you. And may you in turn pass it on to your children. For you are a member of an eternal people, a letter in their scroll. Let their eternity live on in you.

VISION

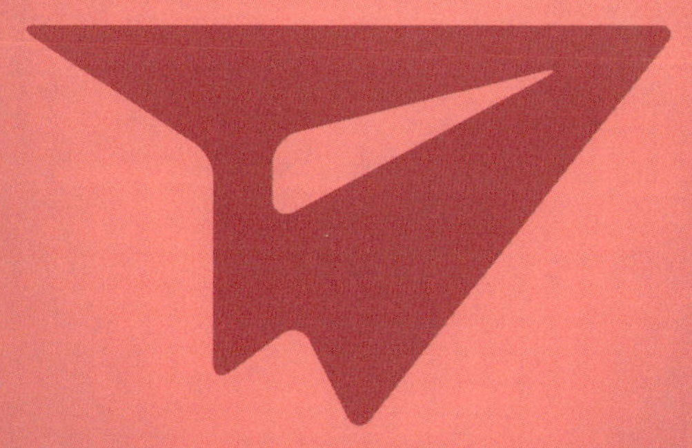

This section is an extended essay originally published in September 2013 under the title *A Judaism Engaged with the World.* This was Rabbi Sacks' final message as chief rabbi before stepping down after more than two decades in office. He recounted his personal journey of discovery and faith. Through a compelling analysis of recent Jewish history, he warns that a Judaism divorced from society will be a Judaism unable to influence others or inspire young Jews. Calling Judaism "the voice of hope in the conversation of humankind," Rabbi Sacks argues for Judaism unafraid to engage with the intellectual, ethical, political, and personal challenges of our time. The essay forms a clarion call to the community to join him in his mission to inspire a new generation of Jewish leaders with the confidence to address the challenges that face Jews, Judaism, and Israel today.

INTRODUCTION TO A JUDAISM ENGAGED WITH THE WORLD

The Jewish Journey: The Next Stage

Judaism is a journey to the future. It is the only civilisation whose golden age, the Messianic Age, is yet to come. As a result, Jews look forward more than they look back.

When Sarah dies, Abraham – by now an old man – mourns her loss, then turns to buying the first Jewish plot of land in Israel and finding a wife for Isaac, his son. He grieves for the past, then without delay proceeds to build the future. At the end of his life, Moses gathers the people, briefly reviews the previous forty years, then delivers an extraordinary series of prophecies about the far horizons of the years ahead.

At the Seder table on Pesaḥ we celebrate history, but we begin and end by talking not about last year but about next year: "Next year we will be free," "Next year in Jerusalem."

When God appears to Moses at the burning bush, first He calls Himself "the God of your father, the God of Abraham, Isaac, and Jacob," the Jewish past. But when asked by Moses for His name, He replies, *Ehyeh asher ehyeh*, "I will be what I will be," I am God whose name is the future tense.

To be a Jew is to keep faith with the past by building a Jewish future. That is the secret of our unbroken capacity through centuries of suffering to renew ourselves as a people. More than we look back, we look forward. So as Elaine and I come to the end of our time in the Chief Rabbinate I want briefly to look back, and then turn to the next stage of the journey.

In 1991 when we began, British Jewry faced a challenge of renewal. The community was shrinking. Outmarriage rates were rising. Jewish life was becoming weaker. We had been losing ten Jews a day every day for forty years. Several outside observers had written that British Jewry was set on a path of slow but inevitable decline. It had a distinguished past. It was unclear whether it had a future.

The way the community responded over the next two decades was extraordinary. Never before in Anglo-Jewish history have more Jewish day schools been built. There is more adult, informal, and family education than ever. Cultural activity has blossomed. There is now a London Jewish Cultural Centre and a Jewish Community Centre is about to open. Synagogues have become centres of community, active throughout the day and week. Services are more informal.

Rabbis no longer wear canonicals, or wardens top hats. Outreach groups thrive. There is less "oy," more joy.

There has been a revolution in community welfare provision: day centres and sheltered housing for the elderly, and more facilities for children and adults with special needs. On moral and social issues the Jewish voice has become a respected part of the national conversation. And thanks to the growth of the *ḥaredi* community, after half a century of year-on-year decline, British Jewry is no longer shrinking but growing. There are more Jewish professionals, facilities, programmes, organisations, and buildings than ever before. Our Victorian predecessors, were they able to see British Jewry today, would stand amazed.

This has been a genuine communal achievement. Thousands of individuals have played a part. In the case of Jewish schools we stand in the debt of those who built and funded them, the teachers, head teachers, and governors who made them centres of excellence, the parents who chose a Jewish education for their children, and the children themselves who have given us pride.

Collectively we owe thanks to the lay leaders, professionals, and volunteers in all the many organisations who have made our community creative, caring, and admired. Head for head, our community gives to Jewish life and the wider society out of all proportion to its numbers. Everyone has contributed, and every contribution made a difference. So, as we end our period of service Elaine and I want to say *Sheheḥeyanu,* thanking God for the privilege of living in such a community at such a time.

Now, looking back then forward, I want to tell the story of my own Jewish journey, why it took me in the direction it did, and why there is a distance yet to go.

The Question

It began, as Jewish journeys often do, with a question. I had arrived at university, the first member of my family to do so. In my memory I see a blur of impressions: undergraduates cycling to lectures, their gowns trailing in the wind, the long tables and oak-panelled walls of the college hall, the ancient stonework of the buildings, the buzz of conversations, and the silence in the college library punctuated only by the slow ticking of a grandfather clock.

Tucked away in a side street, almost completely inconspicuous, was the little synagogue built in the 1930s without a single window facing the street in case, in the fraught atmosphere of the time, fascists would smash the glass and desecrate the place where Jews prayed. It was small, modest, but to the Jewish students it was home. It was there that we ate, there that I encountered cholent for the first time, and there that in the anxious weeks before the Six-Day War we crowded every afternoon to *daven* for the safety of our people and land.

The question that haunted me then, and in one form or another has done so ever since, was: Where were the missing Jews? We who frequented the shul estimated that there were in the region of a thousand Jewish students at the university. Of those, a hundred had some contact with the Jewish Society, and perhaps another fifty who attended the Israel Society. Where were the missing 85 percent? Why weren't they there?

Why was it that, having survived some of the worst tragedies ever to befall a people without abandoning their faith, Jews were doing so now, when there was no serious penalty to be paid for being Jewish? English Jews had waited patiently for almost two hundred years for the right to attend university and obtain a degree. Lionel de Rothschild had been elected four times as member of Parliament for the City of London from 1847 onward, yet did not take his place in the House of Commons for eleven years until he could do so as a Jew without taking a Christian oath. At any time Jews could have abandoned their Judaism and become, like Benjamin Disraeli – converted by his father at the age of six – prime minister of Britain, yet overwhelmingly they did not. Why then were they doing so now?

That was the question: *Where were the missing Jews?*

I started studying Jewish history and quickly realised that what was happening to my generation was not new. It had happened throughout Europe for the previous two centuries. In the nineteenth century, in Russia, Germany, France, and Austria, as the ghetto walls crumbled and Jews entered the wider society, they discovered not a new tolerance but the old prejudice in a new form. In 1879 it was given a new name: antisemitism.

Jews, lacerated by anti-Jewish prejudice, began developing a profound ambivalence about Jewish identity. Mordecai Kaplan best summed it up when he said, "Before the beginning of the nineteenth century all Jews regarded Judaism as a privilege; since then most Jews have come to regard it as a burden."

For more than a century many resolved the conflict by abandoning Judaism. Hundreds of thousands of Jews in central and Eastern Europe converted to Christianity. Heinrich Heine called conversion his entry ticket to European culture. In Vienna as many as 80 percent of Jews registered themselves as *Konfessionsloss*, "of no religion." Many Jews in flight from Eastern Europe to America in the wake of the pogroms abandoned their Jewishness on the boat carrying them across the Atlantic. A famous play, *The Melting Pot*, by Israel Zangwill, ran on Broadway for several years to great acclaim. Its thesis was that in America the old tribal identities that had set Cossack against Jew would disappear. No more Cossacks, no more Jews, just Americans. The missing Jews of my student days were the latest chapter in a story that began long before. Knowing the prejudice that surrounded them, Jews were not sure that they wanted their children or grandchildren to be Jews.

The Inward Turn

Something else happened at about this time that left a deep impression on me. In those days we used to take our holidays on the south coast near Margate, where there was a little shul. In summer the congregation was a mix of locals and holidaymakers much like ourselves. One year, though, a group of Hasidim appeared. They had decided to make it their holiday venue, and they came for many years afterwards.

I had never really met Hasidim before, and it was immediately clear that they saw Jewish identity in quite different terms from the rest of British Jewry. They had no intention of acculturating to English norms, and in the days before multiculturalism, this was a bold statement. They were, and saw themselves as, a group apart. They were numerous, had large families, and were bound to grow as a presence in British Jewish life, especially as other parts of the community seemed to be in decline.

A question came unbidden into my mind: "Is this the beginning of the end of the middle of the road?" It was a good question then. Almost half a century later it still is.

My studies quickly revealed that this response too was born in the nineteenth century. While other Jews were assimilating, some were declining the whole process of Emancipation and acculturation and instead turning inward. That was the path taken by the Jewish communities, especially in Eastern Europe, centred on the yeshiva or the hasidic group.

That world, already waning after the First World War, was almost destroyed in the Holocaust. In one of the greatest reversals in Jewish history, it has now become the fastest-growing element in Israel and throughout the Diaspora. With an intensity of commitment that is nothing short of awe-inspiring, the survivors married and had children and rebuilt their lost communities, growing from *she'erit hapeleta*, a tiny remnant, to become a significant presence in contemporary Jewish life.

So the Jewish world today represents the working through of processes begun in mainland Europe long before the Holocaust. Faced with societies that did not accept them as Jews, a fateful choice framed itself in many Jewish minds: either to enter society and abandon their Jewishness, or to preserve their Jewishness at the cost of turning their back on society. There were, it seemed, just two options: to embrace the wider society and abandon Judaism (assimilation) or to choose Judaism and disengage from the wider society (segregation).

That choice may have made sense in the fraught atmosphere of a mainland Europe dominated by antisemitism from the nineteenth century to the Holocaust. But in the late 1960s, when the State of Israel had just won a stunning victory in the Six-Day War and Jews in the West were living in the most tolerant of times, it made no sense at all.

So in the summer of 1968 I set out on a real journey, to America, to meet as many distinguished rabbis as I could to hear how they understood the Jewish situation of our time.

Encounters

For two months I travelled throughout the United States and Canada, meeting many outstanding Jewish leaders. Wherever I went, two names kept coming up in conversation: Rabbi Joseph Soloveitchik, the greatest Orthodox thinker of the time, and Rabbi Menachem Mendel Schneerson, the Lubavitcher Rebbe. I was determined to meet them both, and despite many obstacles, I did.

They were, in their very different ways, extraordinary men, not least in their willingness to spend time with a young student from across the Atlantic with no real claim on their attention. Those two encounters eventually changed my life. The Rebbe was fully aware of the problem of the missing Jews, especially on campus. He had seen it long before. Already in the early 1950s he had sent emissaries out to work with students, inventing the idea, revolutionary in its time, of Jewish outreach. In our meeting, he challenged me to get personally involved and to take responsibility. Years later I summed up that meeting by saying that good leaders create followers. Great leaders create leaders. The Rebbe challenged me to lead.

Rabbi Soloveitchik challenged me to think. At that time I was studying philosophy, and soon discovered that he was a master in the field. His approach to Jewish philosophy was unlike any I had encountered before. Already in that first meeting he outlined for me the method he had made his own. Jewish philosophy, he said, had to emerge from halakha, Jewish law. Jewish thought and Jewish practice were not two different things but the same thing seen from different perspectives. Halakha was a way of living, a way of thinking about the world – taking abstract ideas and making them real in everyday life.

These were immensely inspiring figures, but what struck me most about them was the depth of their commitment to real engagement with the world. Rabbi Soloveitchik had no fears about the intellectual challenges posed by modern thought. He had studied it widely and deeply and felt no ultimate conflict between the worlds of the yeshiva and the university. The very institution in which he taught – Yeshiva University – defined itself simultaneously as both.

As for the Rebbe, here was a man who had deep relationships with doctors, lawyers, scientists, politicians, academics, writers, people in every sphere of life. His vision was vast, and not only in relation to Jews. He believed that we have a responsibility towards the world as a whole. He often spoke publicly about the *sheva mitzvot benei Noaḥ,* the covenant God made through Noah with all humanity, and believed that Jews should be active in promoting religious values and faith in society, not just within the Jewish community.

So already then as an undergraduate student I had encountered two outstanding figures who were strikingly different from others in their world. Rabbi Soloveitchik represented the yeshiva. The Lubavitcher Rebbe came from the hasidic community. Yet unlike their contemporaries they had turned not inward but outward. They taught that to be good, faithful, practising Jews we needed neither to disengage from society nor fear its challenges.

The Great Divide

Despite their example, the rift I had already glimpsed in the 1960s has become deeper still throughout much of the Jewish world. Today the two most powerful movements in Jewish life are assimilation and segregation. Jews are either engaging with the world at the cost of disengaging from Judaism, or engaging with Judaism at the cost of disengaging from the world.

We are still losing Jews through outmarriage and disaffiliation. Throughout the Diaspora, with minor regional variations, one-half of young Jews is deciding not to have a Jewish marriage, build a Jewish home, and have Jewish children. Each such loss is a tragedy. A family tree that had lasted a hundred generations comes to an end with them. A chain of continuity that held strong for a hundred generations has broken.

Meanwhile, the world of inward-turning, segregationist Orthodoxy is growing at speed. In the summer of

2012, seventy thousand crowded into a baseball stadium to celebrate the completion of *Daf Yomi,* the seven-year cycle of daily Talmud study. Never before in all of history have so many Jews studied at yeshivot – not in the great days of Mir and Volozhin, not even in the academies of Sura and Pumbedita where the Babylonian Talmud was born.

While the two extremes are growing, the centre is shrinking. Jews are either drifting away from mainstream synagogues or starting small, new, breakaway communities. Shuls that once brought together Jews from a wide range of commitment are declining. A certain kind of Jewish identity – proud to be Jewish, proud equally to be an active citizen of the wider society – is waning. In Israel, the split between *ḥaredi* and *ḥiloni,* religious and secular, grows ever deeper. One telling sign is that the sale of ordinary matzot for Pesaḥ is declining. More people are either simply not observing Pesaḥ or are insisting on *matza shemura*. The Jewish world is spinning apart.

As strategies, assimilation and segregation are both dangerous. Throughout history, assimilationists believed that they had solved antisemitism by disappearing. But they hadn't disappeared. They were still recognised and reviled. It happened in Spain in the fifteenth century. It happened in Europe in the nineteenth. Assimilation, the wish to be *kekhol hagoyim,* "like all the nations," is risk laden because it convinces only Jews, not the people they need to convince, that they have become invisible.

Segregation is also dangerous. When you have little to do with the world, you fail to understand it and leave yourself defenceless against it.

Assimilation and segregation may work for individuals, even large numbers of them, but they cannot be the way for the Jewish people as a whole. Not only are they dangerous; they are a failure of nerve in the Judaic project. Can it really be that Judaism has nothing to contribute to society and to the world? Can it be that when Jews engage with the world they have to hide their identity, acting as if they were twenty-first-century equivalents of the Marranos of Spain, Jews in secret but not in public? Are Jewish faith and practice so fragile that they can only be sustained by being screened from all contact with other cultures?

It was once so but it is not so today. The Jewish situation has changed decisively. Israel exists. Jews have a home. In most countries in the Diaspora, Jews are no longer even the most conspicuous minority. *For the first time in four thousand years, Jews have sovereignty and independence in Israel, freedom and equality in the Diaspora.* Shall we act as if we were still in the nineteenth century, not the twenty-first?

The world needs the Jews and Jews need the world. Today for the first time we have the opportunity to live the double truth of that sentence. We must stop feeling defensive about being Jewish and engage with the world with humility but without fear.

The Key Idea: *Kiddush Hashem*

The key concept that has driven me since my encounter with Rabbi Soloveitchik and the Lubavitcher Rebbe has been *kiddush Hashem,* sanctification of God's name. Tragically, often in the past this referred to Jews who died because of their faith. We say they died *al kiddush Hashem.* But what it primarily means is to live in such a way as to inspire respect for God.

When the prophet Isaiah said, in God's name, "You are my witnesses," what he meant was that we have been cast in the role of God's ambassadors to the world. We are commanded to lead our lives so that we become living tutorials in the values Jews first taught the world: the sanctity of life, the dignity of the human person, the twin imperatives of justice and compassion, marriage as a covenant and the home as a sanctuary, community as collective responsibility, the importance of lifelong education, respect for the elderly, and many other ideals that Jews were the first to embrace and of which they are still the great exemplars.

When Dr. Ludwig Guttmann revolutionised the care of paraplegics and created the Paralympics, that was a *kiddush Hashem*. When Viktor Frankl in Auschwitz gave his fellow prisoners the will to live, creating a new psychotherapy based on "man's search for meaning," that was a *kiddush Hashem*. When Jewish economists develop ways of alleviating poverty throughout the developing world, that is a *kiddush Hashem*. When Jewish businesses set new standards in respecting employees, that is a *kiddush Hashem*. When Jews worked with Nelson Mandela to end apartheid or marched with Martin Luther King in the battle for civil rights, that was a *kiddush Hashem*.

The reason is that each of these is a way of showing what God wants from us in this world. He wants us to become His "partners in the work of creation." He wants us to fight the evil men do to one another. He wants us to use our freedom responsibly. He wants us to use our God-given powers to enhance the lives of others.

Judaism was the world's first religion of protest. The exodus in the days of Moses was an unprecedented event: the supreme Power intervening to liberate the supremely powerless. Elsewhere, religion in ancient times was a conservative force. The gods were on the side of the established power. They legitimated hierarchy. They reconciled the masses to a life of ignorance and servitude. How could you challenge the status quo? it was the will of the gods, the structure of the cosmos, on earth as it was in heaven. That is what Karl Marx meant when he called religion the opium of the people.

Judaism opposed this entire constellation of values. It laid the foundations for an egalitarian society based not on equality of wealth or power but on equal access to education, welfare, and human dignity. The prophets never argued that there is injustice, poverty, disease, and violence in the world because that is how God wants it to be. Judaism is God's call to human responsibility, to bring the world closer to the world that ought to be.

That is why Jews are to be found disproportionately as doctors fighting disease, lawyers fighting injustice, educators fighting ignorance, economists fighting poverty, and scientists extending the frontiers of human knowledge. The Greeks believed in fate and gave the world masterpieces of tragedy. Jews believed there is no fate that cannot be averted by penitence, prayer, and charity. Judaism is the principled rejection of tragedy in the name of hope.

Jewish history bears witness to the world that a nation need not be large to be great, nor powerful to be influential. The Jewish people is proof that you can suffer centuries of persecution and exile and still survive and flourish, recovering from every defeat and turning every setback into a matrix of renewal. You can be written off by the world and prove time and again that the world was wrong. Inspired by high ideals and a respect for human dignity, you can outlast any empire. You can suffer and yet sing, walk through the valley of the shadow of death and emerge, limping but undefeated, into the light of new life. Time and again Jews have shown how you can defeat probability by the power of possibility.

The impact of *kiddush Hashem* was always limited in the past because of two factors. For seventeen centuries after the fall of Jerusalem and the destruction of the Second Temple, Jews lived at the margins of society without full civil rights. Then in the nineteenth century they acquired those rights but found themselves in the midst of a vast wave of antisemitism from the Russian pogroms of the 1880s to France of the Dreyfus affair. Few were the places – Britain and America were among the exceptions – where Jews could make their contribution to society as Jews, which is what figures like Sir Moses Montefiore in Britain and Louis Brandeis in America did.

Now it is no longer limited. Israel exists. Jews have equality and respect in most countries of the Diaspora. There is no reason to abandon our Judaism, nor is there reason to turn our back to the world.

Three Models of the Religious Life

In place of assimilation and segregation we need to argue the case for a Judaism that engages with the world. The case is not new. It is set out at the dawn of our history in three striking biblical portraits of Noah, Abraham, and his nephew Lot.

Noah is the only person in Tanakh called a *tzaddik,* "righteous." Yet Noah's righteousness was turned inward. He had no influence on his contemporaries. His was the way of segregation. Hasidim used to call Noah a *tzaddik im peltz,* "a righteous man in a fur coat." There are two ways of keeping warm on a cold day. You can wear a fur coat or light a fire. Wear a fur coat and you warm only yourself. Light a fire and you warm others. Jews are supposed to light a fire.

Lot chose the way of assimilation. He tried to merge into the society, Sodom, in which he had chosen to live. His daughters married local men. We see Lot at the beginning of Genesis 19 sitting at the city gate, implying as Rashi says that he had been appointed a judge. Superficially he seemed to have been accepted. He was soon to discover otherwise. Having welcomed strangers into his house, he found himself surrounded by an angry mob demanding that he hand them over. When he refuses, the mob say, "This one came here as an immigrant, and now all of a sudden, he has set himself up as a judge!" – perhaps the first antisemitic remark in history. When the angels urge him to leave, he delays, fatefully trapped by his own ambivalence as to his real identity. Only when the angels drag him and his daughters out are their lives saved.

Noah and Lot, the exemplars respectively of segregation and assimilation, are not happy precedents. Abraham is different. In Genesis 14 he fights a battle on behalf of the cities of the plain and liberates the people taken hostage. In Genesis 18 he mounts one of the most audacious prayers in history on behalf of the people of Sodom ("Shall the Judge of all the earth not do justice?"). He fights for his neighbours and prays for them but he does not become like them. He lives out the principle that has been the Jewish imperative ever since: Be true to your faith and a blessing to others regardless of their faith.

What is the result? When Abraham comes before the Hittites to buy a plot of land in which to bury Sarah, they say to him: "You are a prince of God in our midst." That is the first instance, and the classic example, of *kiddush Hashem* in the Torah.

Rabbi Samson Raphael Hirsch drew attention to the phrase Abraham used in his prayer to God to save the city.

Perhaps, says Abraham, there are fifty, even ten, *tzaddikim betokh ha'ir*, "righteous people within the city." There is a difference, says Hirsch, between a *tzaddik* and a *tzaddik*-in-the-city. Those who are righteous by separating themselves from the city can save themselves but not others. The challenge is to be righteous within the city, involved in the life of one's contemporaries, working for the good of all. That is the way of Abraham, to live one's faith while engaging with the world.

Abraham's always was the road less travelled. The Sages say that he was called *haIvri*, "the Hebrew," because "he was on one side (*ever eḥad*) while the rest of the world was on the other." Judaism is a countercultural faith, and Jews have often been iconoclasts, willing to challenge the idols of the age.

The assimilationist-segregationist divide in Jewish life today looks less like the way of Abraham, more like the ways respectively of Lot and Noah. There is another way.

What If?

Imagine the following wholly fanciful scenario: that Spinoza, Marx, Freud, Levi-Strauss, Durkheim, Bergson, Wittgenstein, Proust, and Gustav Mahler had all been Jews of faith, comfortable in their identity, speaking in the voice of Jewish tradition, showing the world what it is to engage as a believer-in-God-who-believes-in-us, exemplifying the Jewish values of study, intellect, independence, iconoclasm, *tzedek, mishpat, ḥesed,* and *raḥamim*. They would have been different. The world would have been different. Judaism would have retained its energies instead of losing them to the entropy of an undifferentiated world.

That is what philosophy calls a counterfactual conditional. In Hebrew we say *Halevai*. Would that it were, but it wasn't. What I am arguing, though, is something else. *The two dominant strands in the Jewish world today are fighting the battles of the past, not those of the future.*

Assimilation made sense in the nineteenth and twentieth centuries, in a Jewish world traumatised by antisemitism. It makes no sense at all today, either in Israel or in the multicultural democracies of the West. In the United States, where outmarriage continues at the rate of one in two, Harvard sociologist Robert Putnam has shown that Jews are the group more respected and admired than any other.

Segregation made immense sense after the Holocaust, when the heartlands of tradition in Eastern Europe had been almost entirely obliterated. But today, by a miracle of rebirth, the *ḥaredi* community is stronger than it was before the start of the Second World War. It has won the battle. We are in its debt. By sheer commitment and dedication it has brought the worlds of Jewish learning and practice back to life. Now is the time to turn outward and share its energies with the rest of the Jewish world.

The battle of the twenty-first century is the one Jews have been waiting for, for at least two thousand years. What if we had a Jewish state and could do what Jews have been commanded to do since the days of Moses: build a society based on Torah values of righteousness, justice, kindness, and compassion, the great prophetic virtues?

What if non-Jews no longer looked down on Judaism as inferior to Christianity, Islam, or enlightenment universalism? What if they actually respected it as a source of wisdom and inspiration?

These are no longer "What if?" They are the actuality within which we live. Sometimes the Jewish world can seem like a group of passengers on a train who are arguing with such passion that they entirely fail to notice that the train has reached its destination and it is time to get out. That is what happens when we forget that Judaism does not mean living in the past. It means living with the past, but with eyes firmly turned towards the future.

Imagine a Judaism that engaged our greatest minds, our top professionals, our leading businesspeople, our most creative artists, musicians, and film producers, encouraging them to go out into the world making a Jewish contribution as role models and exemplars of faith – the faith in God that leads us to have faith in the possibility of defeating the reign of violence, terror, injustice, and oppression – a Judaism that might have led the missing 85 percent of my contemporaries to be proud to be Jews.

This is not mere imagining. One of the privileges of being a chief rabbi is that you get the chance to road test ideas in the real world. For more than two decades I tried to see whether it was possible to bring a Jewish voice to the public conversation, showing that Judaism has insights, compelling not just to Jews but non-Jews also, into politics, economics, civil society, philosophy, psychology, and global ethics. Could we take the best scientific and philosophical wisdom of our time and use it to develop new insights into Torah? Could a religious figure engage in public dialogue with leading intellectuals of the age without being defensive on the one hand, or dismissive on the other? Could you connect leaders of the modern world who happen to be Jews, with their Judaism, getting them to see that their commitments are, whether they know it or not, part of our collective heritage? I tried these things and found that the answer in each case was "Yes."

I discovered how much non-Jews admire Judaism and are lifted by it. We are admired by others for the strength of our families and the support of our communities; for our love of education and the life of the mind; for our commitment to philanthropy and social responsibility; and for our ability to combine reverence for the past with sensitivity to the present and responsibility to the future. *I discovered that non-Jews respect Jews who respect Judaism. Non-Jews are embarrassed by Jews who are embarrassed by Judaism.*

I also discovered how enthusiastically young Jews resonate to this message. They want to contribute to the wider society and to humanity as a whole. They are not inspired by a Judaism that speaks constantly of antisemitism, the Holocaust, the isolation of Israel, and the politics of fear. Nor are they inspired by a Judaism that asks them to look down on, and sever all contacts with, the world. Jews are in the forefront of almost every endeavour today. How transformative it would be if they did so as Jews, ambassadors of the Divine Presence, living Jewish lives, energised by Jewish texts, sustained by Jewish prayers, driven to share our legacy of hope. It would be the greatest *kiddush Hashem* in history.

Likewise in Israel. I am repeatedly astonished by how warmly secular Jews – self-defined *ḥilonim* – respond to a Judaism that speaks in the language of prophetic ideals, not that of politics and power; that relates to them with non-judgmental love; that values their contributions to the Jewish world; that lifts them instead of putting them down. I travel the world, speaking to many groups of many faiths in many countries, and among the most responsive audiences of all are secular Israelis. This led me to conclude that secular Israelis are wrong in thinking that secular Israelis are secular. They are *maaminim benei maaminim,* "believers, the children of believers," who have simply not yet encountered a Judaism that speaks to them.

The challenge of our time is to go out to Jews with a Judaism that relates to the world – their world – with intellectual integrity, ethical passion, and spiritual power, a Judaism neither intimidated by the world nor dismissive of it, a Judaism fully expressive of the broad horizons and high ideals of our heritage. There is no contradiction, not even a conflict, between contributing to humanity and affirming our distinctive identity. *To the contrary: by being what only we are, we contribute to the world what only we can give.*

We have much to teach the world – and the world has much to teach us. It is essential that we do so with generosity and humility. I have called Judaism the voice of hope in the conversation of humankind. Our ability to survive some of the worst tragedies any people has known without losing our faith in life itself; to suffer and yet rebuild; to lose and yet recreate; to honour the past without being held captive by the past – all of which are embodied today in the State of Israel, living symbol of the power of hope – are vitally important not just to ourselves but to the world.

In the twenty-first century, Jews will need the world, and the world will need the Jews. We will not win the respect of the world if we ourselves do not respect the world: if we look down on non-Jews and on Jews less religious than ourselves. Nor will we win the respect of the world if we do not respect ourselves and our own distinctive identity. Now more than ever the time has come for us to engage with the world as Jews, and we will find that our own world of mind and spirit will be enlarged.

Akavya ben Mahalalel

Twenty-two years ago, on a stiflingly hot day, I stood in the St John's Wood synagogue to be inducted by my predecessor Lord Jakobovits as chief rabbi of the United Hebrew Congregations of the Commonwealth. Many thoughts went through my mind: thanks to God for the privilege of serving so distinguished a community of communities, to my parents for the love of Judaism and the Jewish people they had taught me, and to Elaine for accompanying me on this new and challenging stage of our journey together.

I spoke, that day, about Jewish renewal and creativity and much else beside. But one sentence kept running through my mind and became the underlying theme of my speech – the remark of the second-century teacher R. Akavya ben Mahalalel, who taught his disciples never to forget three things: "Where you are coming from, where you are going to, and before whom you are accountable."

It seems like a trite remark, hardly worth saying, let alone repeating. But Akavya ben Mahalalel was anything but a conventional teacher. The Mishna (Eduyot 5:6) tells us that he held tenaciously to his own interpretation of the tradition even though he was opposed by the majority of his colleagues. Having failed to get him to change his views by conventional means, they tried to persuade him by the promise of promotion. They would appoint him *av beit din*, head of the rabbinic court, they said, if only he would retract. His reply was magnificent: "I would rather be called a fool all my lifetime than a sinner (who compromised his views for the sake of personal advancement) for one moment."

One tradition says that he was excommunicated. Despite this the Mishna says that "the Temple gates never closed behind a man in Israel as great in wisdom and fear of sin as Akavya ben Mahalalel." Whether it was the Lubavitcher Rebbe or Rabbi Soloveitchik or, *lehavdil ben ḥayim leḥayim*, my own teacher Rabbi Dr. Nachum Rabinovitch, I have always been drawn to rabbis like Akavya who stood out against the consensus of their contemporaries.

What Akavya was saying, I think, is that though the Torah is timeless, we live in time. To be a Jew is to be part of a journey begun four thousand years ago when Abraham and Sarah, responding to a heavenly call, left their land, birthplace, and family to travel to an unknown destination, there to begin an experiment in living that has summoned us ever since. That journey defines Jewish time. We do not simply live in the present. We are guardians of our people's past and shapers of its future, and both are essential. It is not enough to remember "where you are coming from." We have also to remember "where you are going to." Yesterday's battles are not today's, and we fight today's for the sake of tomorrow. As I put it in the course of one of the most important battles we fought in British Jewry, the key question we had to ask was not "Did we have Jewish grandparents?" but "Will we have Jewish grandchildren?"

British Jewry has responded magnificently to the challenge. The new schools we have built, the cultural creativity British Jewry now shows, and the higher profile we have in the public square, will, I believe, mean that we will have more Jewish grandchildren than might otherwise have been the case. I could not live with myself, however, if I did not continue to do everything in my power to try to make Judaism more compelling for the next generation, intellectually, ethically, and spiritually. We must be prepared to engage with the world unashamedly and uncompromisingly as Jews. Otherwise we will find yet again that the choice will be either to assimilate or segregate, leaving no one left to challenge the world or make a contribution to it as a Jew.

The world is now global and we need to act globally, because what is happening in Britain and the Commonwealth is happening elsewhere as well. So I have decided to go back to where I began, teaching, writing, broadcasting, and using new media, trying to inspire Jews of all ages and backgrounds to engage with the world as Jews, abandoning neither their Jewishness nor the world. Judaism is more than equal to all the challenges of the contemporary world, and it is an essential voice in the human conversation.

The question I asked forty-five years ago – *Where are the missing Jews?* – still moves me to remind others what centuries of antisemitism made us forget, that we are bearers of the Divine Presence, witnesses in ourselves to something far greater than ourselves, living proof of the dignity of difference and of the power of faith to heal a fractured world. *The world needs the Jews, and Jews need the world.* That is the *tzav hashaa,* the imperative of our time, and there is much for us to do.

It has been a huge privilege, these past twenty-two years, to serve British and Commonwealth Jewry, as well as engaging with Israel, American Jewry, and other communities around the world. During that time Elaine and I have been humbled by the talent, energy, drive, and dedication that exist throughout this great community of communities. It is as if Jews know intuitively that to live is to give. We are the people whose numbers are small but whose contributions are vast, and that is what makes us agents of hope, each in our own way.

I was blessed by having a distinguished predecessor, Lord Jakobovits of blessed memory, and I feel equally blessed to have a fine successor, Rabbi Ephraim Mirvis. Elaine and I now begin the next stage of our journey. May God continue to bless our community and people, and may we continue collectively to be a source of blessing to the world.

I end twenty-two years of service to British Jewry feeling younger and more energised than I was when I began. Now I begin the next challenge: to try to inspire a new generation of Jewish leaders, to deepen the conversation between Torah and the wisdom of the world, and to do so globally. Where it will lead, I do not know. But to be a Jew is to continue the journey, honouring the past by building the future for which they prayed.

About the Author

Rabbi Lord Jonathan Sacks (1948–2020) was a global religious leader, philosopher, award-winning author, and respected moral voice. He was the laureate of the 2016 Templeton Prize in recognition of his "exceptional contributions to affirming life's spiritual dimension." Described by HM King Charles III as "a light unto this nation" and by former British Prime Minister Sir Tony Blair as "an intellectual giant," Rabbi Sacks was a frequent and sought-after contributor to radio, television, and the press, both in Britain and around the world.

After achieving first-class honours in philosophy at Gonville and Caius College, Cambridge, he pursued post-graduate studies in Oxford and London, gaining his doctorate in 1981 and receiving rabbinic ordination from Jews' College and Yeshivat Etz Chaim. He served as the rabbi of Golders Green Synagogue and Marble Arch Synagogue in

London before becoming principal of Jews' College (now the London School of Jewish Studies).

He served as Chief Rabbi of the United Hebrew Congregations of the Commonwealth for twenty-two years, between 1991 and 2013. He held seventeen honorary degrees, including a Doctor of Divinity conferred to mark his first ten years in office as chief rabbi, by the then Archbishop of Canterbury, Lord Carey.

In recognition of his work, Rabbi Sacks won several international awards, including the Jerusalem Prize in 1995 for his contribution to Diaspora Jewish life, the Ladislaus Laszt Ecumenical and Social Concern Award from Ben-Gurion University in Israel in 2011, the Guardian of Zion Award from the Ingeborg Rennert Center for Jerusalem Studies at Bar-Ilan University, and the Katz Award in recognition of his contribution to the practical analysis and application of halakha in modern life in Israel in 2014. He was knighted by Her Majesty Queen Elizabeth II in 2005 and made a Life Peer, taking his seat in the House of Lords in October 2009.

The author of more than forty books, Rabbi Sacks published a new English translation and commentary for the *Koren Sacks Siddur,* the first new Orthodox siddur in a generation, as well as powerful commentaries for the *Rosh HaShana, Yom Kippur, Pesaḥ, Shavuot,* and *Sukkot Maḥzorim*. A number of his books have won literary awards. *Not in God's Name,* was awarded a 2015 National Jewish Book Award in America and was a top ten *Sunday Times* bestseller in the UK. Others include *The Dignity of Difference,* winner of the Grawemeyer

Award in Religion in 2004 for its success in defining a framework for interfaith dialogue between people of all faiths and of none, and National Jewish Book Awards for *A Letter in the Scroll* in 2000, *Covenant & Conversation: Genesis* in 2009, and the *Koren Sacks Pesaḥ Maḥzor* in 2013. His *Covenant & Conversation* commentaries on the weekly Torah portion, which are translated into numerous languages, including Hebrew, Spanish, Portuguese, and Turkish, are read in Jewish communities around the world.

Rabbi Sacks was married to Elaine for fifty years. They have three children and several grandchildren.

www.rabbisacks.org / @RabbiSacks

Maggid Books
The best of contemporary Jewish thought
from Koren Jerusalem